GUILT BY ASSOCIATION

GUILT BY ASSOCIATION

▼

A Survival Guide for Homeowners, Board Members and Property Managers
Second Edition

Jordan I. Shifrin

Writers Club Press
San Jose New York Lincoln Shanghai

Guilt By Association
A Survival Guide for Homeowners,
Board Members and Property Managers
Second Edition

Writers Club Press
an imprint of iUniverse.com, Inc.

For information address:
iUniverse.com, Inc.
5220 S 16th, Ste. 200
Lincoln, NE 68512
www.iuniverse.com

ISBN: 0-595-19812-0

Printed in the United States of America

CONTENTS

Acknowledgements vii

Preface ix

Legal Authority xiii

Chapter 1 Purchasing a Unit 1

Chapter 2 Developer to Homeowner Control:
           Turnover of the New Association 7

Chapter 3 The Annual Meeting 17

Chapter 4 Once You Are on the Board 29

Chapter 5 Executive or Closed Sessions 32

Chapter 6 Sweetheart Contracts 37

Chapter 7 Steps to Consider When Addressing Developer Defects 44

Chapter 8 Selecting Contractors 51

Chapter 9 Adopting a Budget 55

Chapter 10 Reserve or Borrow: Capital Expenditures
            and Deferred Maintenance 60

Chapter 11 Recommended Procedures for Keeping
            Minutes for Property Owners' Associations 64

Chapter 12 Adopting Rules and Regulations 70

Chapter 13 Risks and Liabilities for Property Managers 77

Chapter 14 Insurance 82

Chapter 15 Board Members or Bored Members:
            How to Recruit and Retain Good People for
            Condominium and Homeowner Association Boards 89

Chapter 16 Using Committees: Or How Not to Do It All Yourself 95
Chapter 17 The Role of the Association Attorney:
           Representing the Board 100
Chapter 18 Dealing With A Crisis: The Lawyer's Role 108
Chapter 19 Keeping Your Legal Expenses Under Control 112
Chapter 20 Access To Association Records 116
Chapter 21 Tools For A Better Board Meeting;
           Why Do These People Act This Way? 121
Chapter 22 Collection Policy and Procedures for
           Condominiums and Homeowners Associations 125
Chapter 23 First Right of Refusal for Condominiums:
           Protection or Illusion 131
Chapter 24 Leasing Units 140
Chapter 25 Employment Practices for
           Associations and Management 145
Chapter 26 Boards & Managers: Partners or Adversaries 151
Chapter 27 Umbrella Associationvs.
           Residential Association Responsibility 156
Chapter 28 Man's Best Friend?The Association's Worst Enemy 160
Chapter 29 Procedures for Conducting Informal and
           Administrative Hearings for Cooperatives,
           Condominiums and Homeowners Associations 164
Conclusion 169
About the Author 171

Acknowledgements

I would like to thank my family, my partners, my staff and most of all my secretary, Eileen Digmann, for without their cooperation and support, this book would not have been possible.

This book is dedicated to the thousands of property professionals, volunteer Board members and active owners I have worked with over the years, who perform their tasks tirelessly. They are overworked, under compensated and rarely appreciated, yet they help perpetuate a lifestyle that makes home ownership a reality for millions of people across the country.

Jordan I. Shifrin
1995

PREFACE

This book can serve as a how_to guide for anyone living in a cooperative or condominium or belonging to a home-owners association and/or serving on the Board. Through representing associations as legal counsel since 1977, I have learned many things, both legal as well as practical, about operating an association.

In 1975, as a new homeowner and second_year law student, I reluctantly agreed to serve on an "ad_hoc" committee of homeowners prior to the developer turning over control of our association to a Board of Directors. The developer had raised assessments from \$30 to \$35 per month causing a community_wide uprising. The first meeting was held in a driveway and seven representatives were selected. Since I was the only person in attendance wearing a suit, I was appointed chairman!

We met monthly for more than a year, until the developer held an election for the first Board. By then I had taken a class in condominium law, graduated from law school and joined a national organization for associations.

Since my mother did not raise a fool, I did not run for the first Board of Directors, because I had already decided that this association could be my first client. This prophecy came to pass, and with an hourly billing rate of $25.00 per hour, I was ready to make my way in the world.

Over the years, I have worked with thousands of people and read enough declarations that if laid end to end would…be a lot of declarations! Needless to say, I have worked with some of the most dedicated and hardworking individuals one could ever encounter.

An association can represent either a cross_section of the population or a homogenous ethnic or age group. The members elect a governing Board that operates as a unit of local government: It administers the day_to_day affairs of millions of dollars worth of real property, passes and enforces laws and runs a business that is funded by assessments paid by the members.

In most instances, the people who volunteer or are drafted for a position on the Board do not have one minute's worth of experience in this area. Most Boards consist primarily of lay people who must wrestle with solving a myriad of problems while dealing with owners, contractors, lawyers, accountants, insurance workers, municipal governments and so on.

I have always looked at my primary function as that of a teacher. By applying a smattering of legal theory, reinforced by years of experience and the ability to read badly written documents, as well as a little common sense tempered with a sense of humor, I have helped many Boards achieve their goal of self_government, at least until the Board members all resign or sell their units and we start the process over again.

This book contains a compilation of articles I have written over the years to help Boards address their day_to_day problems from a legal, as well as a practical, point of view. I hope you find it helpful.

Jordan I. Shifrin
August 1995

LEGAL AUTHORITY

Associations are created either by statute or by contract. A statute, such as the Illinois General Not For Profit Corporation Act, may set out very basic requirements for structuring the Board, but rights and responsibilities are always elaborated on in greater detail in the covenants and by_laws. The legal authority (power) of associations is derived from the following components:

1. **Declaration.** The declaration, which contains the basic legal structure for the association, defines its powers and sets forth the rights of the members. The contents of a declaration of condominium also must contain certain essential elements and is supplemented and superseded by the Illinois Condominium Property Act.

2. **Articles of Incorporation.** If the association or cooperative is a corporation, articles of incorporation (corporate charter) must be executed and filed with the Secretary of State. In Illinois, a condominium association is deemed to be a not_for_profit corporation even if it has not filed articles with the Secretary of State [§18.3]. Some cooperatives are incorporated as regular corporations.

3.   **By_Laws**. The by_laws of an association contain the basic rules for governing the Board. To some extent the by_laws may duplicate what is found in the declaration, although the by_laws should be easier to amend. Unfortunately, they often have the same requirements as the declaration or, in the worst case, are incorporated as part of the declaration. The by_laws may be slightly different for an unincorporated association than they are for an incorporated association. However, the Board members could lose some of the statutory protections and indemnities if the association is not incorporated and in good standing.

4.   **State Statutes**. Extensive statutory provisions govern the creation of associations and the administration and operation of the association of owners. Those responsible for the operation of the association are affected in some way by state statute. For example, the Illinois General Not For Profit Corporation Act sets out the basic requirements for the operation of corporate boards, which covers all condominium associations, most homeowners associations and some cooperatives. Numerous other statutes (Human Rights Act, Revenue Act, etc.) have provisions that impact associations as well.

5.   **Local Ordinances**. Local ordinances and codes may apply to owners associations. Residential and commercial projects are subject to zoning regulations, building codes, health and safety ordinances, parking and traffic restrictions and regulations, and sometimes resale regulations and

conversion restrictions. Many local governments have consumer protection legislation, as well.

6. **Federal Statutes.** A number of federal statutes and federal agencies impact owners associations. The Federal National Mortgage Association (FNMA), Federal Home Loan Mortgage Corporation (FHLMC), Federal Housing Administration (FHA) and Veterans Administration (VA) affect associations in the area of financing. The Internal Revenue Code, of course, applies to the income received by owners associations. Other regulatory laws, such as the Condominium Abuse and Relief Act, the Fair Housing Amendments Act of 1989, etc., also impact association policy.

7. **Rules and Regulations.** Although last in order of priority, the rules often are given the highest consideration by courts of law. It is most important for an association to have specifically drawn, updated rules in the hands of every owner and resident in order to control behavior and maintain the lifestyle of an association. Generally adopted by the Board, these rules should be reviewed and revised annually to stay current with the law and changes in the community.

Board members and managers should always be familiar with the general requirements of their operating documents and governing laws; however, interpretation and application should be left to the association's attorney. Board members and managers who attempt to practice law without a license can cost an association thousands of dollars by either misapplying or misinterpreting their authority or by being in the middle of a conflict situation.

8. **Case Law.** In addition to the statutes and governing documents, associations are also subject to court decisions at the state and federal level. Case law precedent is referred to as "common law." All court decisions rendered at an Appellate level subject Boards and associations to additional levels of authority. Although Illinois state law and federal decisions take precedence, when there is no Illinois case of record, a court will look at other states as well.

9. **Scholarly Treatises.** Articles, books, treatises, etc., written by experts can be used in association governance when no other authority or guidelines exist, i.e., setting a formula to collect reserves.

10. **Amending Documents.** The authority to amend a legal document is contained in the document itself. There may be certain restrictions on the amendment process, some of which may arise from state law or local ordinance. Generally such restrictions will be referred to in the legal documents themselves, although not always. Some villages require municipal approval of any proposed amendment, as well as owner approval.

CHAPTER I

▼

PURCHASING A UNIT

For many people, the purchase of a condominium, town-home or co_op will be the most significant financial decision of their life. A properly conducted transaction and, more importantly, what happens after it is completed may have a long_range effect on their economic well_being.

A real estate closing should go very smoothly, and the attorney's fees should be viewed as part of the total investment. When a dispute arises, it is important to resolve it prior to the time of closing. This is why it is essential to have an objective and experienced professional resolving the controversy. In most cases, a closing is a very emotional experience, especially for a first_time buyer.

In a number of states, title insurance companies and/or escrow companies control all aspects of the real estate "settlement," exclusive of any input from a lawyer. Unless a "legal" problem arises, a lawyer's participation is unwarranted. In Illinois, however, custom dictates that lawyers have a significant role in the conduct of a closing. The author's philosophy has always been that a conscientious practitioner can save his or her client a great deal of aggravation and substantial sums of money by merely practicing "preventive law." In other words, take 10 steps down the road and then look back to see from whence you came. Following are some basic areas to review prior to buying a condominium, townhome or co_op.

Learning about the Property

Are you looking for a townhome, a co_op, a condominium apartment? Do you want a pool, exercise room, laundry facilities, etc.

Whether you are buying new construction, working with a realtor or driving around looking at "FOR SALE BY OWNER" properties, it is important to know what type of community you are buying into.

Are pets allowed? Can you rent out your property? Can you buy additional parking spaces? Always do a diligent inquiry before you sign an offer to purchase. The "culture" of each association may not be universally suitable for every purchaser.

Coordinating with the Realtor(s)

Most transactions have two or more real estate salespeople involved. It is important for the attorneys and the brokers to work together as a team. Remember, everyone's objective is the same—to close the deal.

Some people forget that a real estate transaction is not intended to be an adversary proceeding. Through frequent communication, problems regarding occupancy dates, walk_ through items, appropriate credits and all other potential trouble spots can be resolved at a preliminary stage.

The salesperson should make sure that the purchaser's attorney has the following items: a copy of the purchase agreement, any riders attached, applications for financing, all association documents in the seller's possession, the seller's attorney's name, etc. Then the purchaser's attorney can immediately "touch base" with all of the principals to begin preparing the way for a smooth transaction, even if it is not scheduled for two months. If the property is new construction, then all of the aforestated information can be obtained from the builder.

Reviewing the Contract

Your attorney should always review the agreement prior to consummating a final deal. If he or she does not review the contract prior to final acceptance, "The horse may already be out of the barn when the door is closed."

Most standard form agreements prepared by title companies, real estate associations, etc., are generally seller–oriented. An experienced real estate lawyer should be familiar with these forms. The attorney must make sure his or her client has enough time to obtain financing, the buyer is not paying any charges that are customarily seller's charges, the seller or builder warranties the condition of the premises, a current survey of the property is provided, etc. In Illinois, under §22.1 of the Illinois Condominium Property Act, upon request a seller also must provide a copy of the declaration, by_laws, operating budget, a floor plan (new construction only), a statement of liens and accounting status, anticipated capital expenditures for the next two years, status of reserve funds, financial statement, status of any pending litigation, insurance coverage, a statement of improvements and alterations to the unit and the name of the principal officer or agent of the association. This information must be provided within 30 days of a written request and the association has the right to charge a fee for copies. If the property is a conversion condominium, the developer also must provide a statement of any condominium fee due, a statement of actual expenditures made for repairs within the last two years, a statement of provisions made for reserves and an engineer's report. Also, many communities have adopted consumer protection conversion ordinances which may require additional disclosure.

In Illinois, the seller of any real property must fill out an affidavit disclosing the existence of any material defects.

Review Financing Documents

In this age of complex financing arrangements and "unconventional" mortgages, it is important to be informed about what type of financing obligation you are incurring. The attorney should be consulted prior to a buyer paying any application fees in advance. Questions such as the following must be considered: Is the mortgage adjustable? Is there a balloon payment? To what standard is the interest rate linked? How many points is the mortgage broker charging? Will HUD adjust the proposed rate of interest prior to closing? Is there a minimum owner/occupancy requirement?

The lawyer must be sure that the note, mortgage and all condominium documents are prepared in strict compliance with the law. Most closings now provide for execution of loan documents at the time of closing (settlement). However, a diligent attorney should review copies of all documents prior to the closing.

Long_Range Planning

Should you take title to the property in a trust? Although the benefits and detriments of trusts are dependent on your particular needs, it is important to review the necessity of taking title and how to eventually accept title.

Reviewing the Documents

Does the survey show the property is free and clear of encroachments? Do the boundaries and building lines conform to local ordinances? Are all of the title exceptions noted? Is the deed made out properly? Have the expenses and credits been properly apportioned? Has the seller disclosed all regular and special assessments?

Remember, in a condominium, since exterior modifications do not affect clear title, the building survey is often available only at great expense. As long as the title insurance company and lender accept this situation, it is not an essential document.

By taking just a few minutes to carefully scrutinize each document, your attorney can ensure that you are getting what you have bargained for. Remember, if an attorney does not methodically review the documents, who will?

The Closing (Settlement)

After following the above recommendations and communicating with the brokers, lawyer, lender, title company, builder (if applicable) and buyer, the closing need be only a mere formality. Most major problems can be solved in advance of the closing.

Last_minute changes, review of closing figures and resolving final details are the only additional tasks other than exchanging documents and dispersing funds. At the time of closing, the attorney should make sure that the recorded documents and policy of title insurance are forwarded to his or her office for final review prior to being sent to the client. All documents should be carefully and thoroughly explained to the client to assure that he or she understands what has transpired.

Conclusion

This chapter details some of an attorney's responsibilities in the course of representing a real estate purchaser. The attorney's primary role will be to protect his or her client's interest and, notwithstanding the solitary transaction, possibly establish a long_term attorney_client relationship. Most importantly, your new home will not become a nest of problems after the fact.

CHAPTER 2

▼

DEVELOPER TO HOMEOWNER CONTROL: TURNOVER OF THE NEW ASSOCIATION

The power to operate and administer a condominium or homeowners association lies with the Board of Directors. The most common misunderstanding among new unit owners is that at some point after they buy, the developer will "create" an association. Another common misconception is that if the unit owners "join" this association they will lose all of their rights against the developer for various wrongs and the developer will leave and not have any further liability. Nothing could be further from the truth!

The process of transferring control from the developer to the homeowners is required by law and in the owners' best interests, with long_term consequences for the association. Following is a step_by_step process outlining this transition.

1.   Developer_Controlled Board

Section 18.2 of the Illinois Condominium Property Act, as well as most declarations, dictates that the rights and privileges held and performed by the developer must be imposed on a Board of Directors When the developer initially records the declaration and by_laws for the association, the association is created. Once the first units are occupied, the association must now function through a Board of Directors to administer and maintain the common areas.

In theory, the developer is supposed to elect a Board during the beginning stages of developing and selling the properties. However, most developers operate without the formality of a Board approving decisions. This presents a potential for conflicts of interest. The developer mainly is interested in a quick turnover of unsold units, which translates into low assessments and minimal reserves. Generally, the reserve is established by the initial purchasers after each buyer deposits the equivalent of several months' assessments. This payment is to be held aside at closing by the developer and later turned over to the association. Some unscrupulous developers may attempt to run development expenses through the association operating account or not pay their fair share of assessments on the unsold units. They may also attempt to dip into this reserve to cover shortfalls.

In most cases, it is merely a matter of maintaining a loose and informal structure, and individual decision making. However, most experienced developers will retain a professional management company at an early stage, which will facilitate a smoother operation.

On the other hand, some developers will designate a representative to operate the association who is obviously looking out for the developer's interests rather than the homeowners'. Since a Board of Directors is deemed to act in a fiduciary capacity relative to the owners, this compounds the potential for conflicts of interest.

In a perfect world, the developer will appoint several interested homeowners to sit on a Board with the developer's representatives to begin the process of transferring control. However, all too often, the transfer of responsibility does not take place until the first annual meeting of members of the association.

2.   **Ad_Hoc Committees**

While the developer is operating the association, some owners may become frustrated with the progress toward completing certain projects or the general way things get done. A small group of owners should begin to meet independently to act as a transition team to assume control when the time comes. Management companies can help by seeking out intelligent, business_oriented people to form such committees.

The committee can initiate future planning, meet with the developer, become familiar with contracts, provide input for budgeting and generally become educated in association operations. Ideally, group members will have enough experience and name recognition so that at the first meeting of association members, they will be assured of election to the Board.

Remember, the type of people elected to the first Board will have a significant effect on how the association functions in the future.

3.   First Annual Meeting of Members

Contrary to popular notion, this meeting called by the developer does not "create" the association. As previously stated, the association is already in existence, even if it is administered passively. Section 18.3 of the Illinois Condominium Property Act ("Act") holds an association and its Board to the standards of an Illinois Not_For_Profit Corporation, even if the developer neglected to have the association incorporated.

The election of the initial Board of a condominium or a master association must take place no later than 60 days after the sale of 75% of the units, or three years after recording the declaration, whichever is earlier (§18.2(b) of the Act). Some homeowner and master association declarations require 100% of the units to be sold, with no time restrictions.

Once this deadline passes, the developer must notify owners that it is time to hold a meeting of members to elect a Board. Although the statute does not contain penalties for failure to do so, a court order would be relatively easy to obtain, based upon a violation of the statute.

A notice must be sent out announcing the time and place of the meeting, not less than 10 days nor more than 30 days in advance. Generally, proxies, nominating petitions and other materials are sent out, but I have seen elections conducted from the floor with hand votes, even though written ballots are required.

Usually there is a small group of active homeowners who have been involved with the association prior to this time that forms a core to elect to the Board (see Ad_Hoc Committees). At the meeting, a Board is elected and the transfer of power "symbolically" takes place. The books, records and moneys are transferred over a period of time and not necessarily at the meeting itself. The officers are elected by the Board members, not the owners, at a subsequent Board meeting (sometimes held the same evening after the owners' meeting).

Once the Board is elected, it will need to have several organizational meetings to set up procedures and rules within a short time.

4.   **The First Year**

The first year is critical in the planning and operation of an association. The following steps must be taken immediately to assure a successful beginning:

A.   The Board elects officers.

B.   The Board selects or reaffirms management. Whether it is the Board itself, an individual or a professional company, financial management must commence immediately. Even if a Board is self_managing, independent financial consultation must be sought to guarantee establishing proper proceedings and to avoid the appearance of impropriety.

C.   The Board selects legal counsel. A qualified and experienced attorney must be selected. A Board, in fulfilling its dual role of operating a business funded by other people's money and running a government (passing and administering laws), must have access to competent advice when questions arise. Because Board members are potentially exposed to personal liability, they should seek to hire an attorney who is experienced in dealing with community associations to get the right answers.

D.   The Board selects an accountant. A prompt review of all financial records is a must at the initial stage of the Board's control. A qualified, experienced accountant can determine whether the developer has paid its fair share and that all moneys are properly accounted for.

E.   The   Board   establishes   committees. Standing committees that act as advisory commissions to the Board will make the Board's job much easier. Buildings and grounds, finance, recreation, rules and regulations, etc., are some areas well suited to committee formation. The committees are also the logical training ground for future Board members.

F.   In addition, the new Board should be looking to implement the following tasks:

  (1) Adopt rules and regulations.
  (2) Review working drawings and punchlists for unremedied builder defects.
  (3) Review all existing contracts to assure that they are up to date and performed satisfactorily.
  (4) Conduct a walk_through of all common areas.
  (5) Engage an architectural/engineering firm to inspect the buildings and common areas and assist in preparing a reserve study.
  (6) Review all insurance coverage with the insurance company's representative.
  (7) Establish strict policies on the frequency and conduct of Board meetings.

Once all of the foregoing areas are addressed and procedures are in place for a smooth and efficiently operating association, the Board will be able to fulfill its primary objectives, i.e., to preserve, protect and enhance property values, maintain the quality of life for its members and act on their behalf to promote the safety and welfare of the property.

ITEMS OR COPIES NEEDED FOR ATTOR-NEY'S FILES AT
THE TIME AN ASSOCIATION TURNS OVER FROM DEVELOPER TO HOMEOWNER CONTROL

1. Certificate and articles of incorporation (original recorded copies preferred)
2. Declaration, by_laws, rules and regulations plus all amendments to each (original recorded copies preferred)
3. Master insurance policies plus date of, term, company and underwriter
4. Current list of unit owners, unit numbers and addresses
5. Management contract
6. Tax returns, if any
7. Tax I.D. number (Employer I.D. number) from the IRS
8. Minutes of association meetings
9. Minutes of Board meetings plus all resolutions passed
10. Any amendments to rules and regulations
11. List of contracts or agreements executed by association with summary of the term and amount of each contract, or copies of same, and summary of any verbal employment agreements
12. List of certificates waiving right of first refusal, date given and to whom
13. Statement of the reserve account—bank, interest, amount expended and received
14. Correspondence with members regarding enforcement, default and statements of resolution of disputes handled by the Board

15. Newsletters and other general communications to all members from the Board
16. List of litigation items, including collections instituted and suits against the association
17. Member or association complaints and claims against the developer and any resolution thereof
18. Any notices of state or municipal action affecting the association
19. Date and time of official inspections of association, including swimming pool
20. List of property tax index numbers, preferably copies of old bills
21. Plat for entire PUD
22. Correspondence with title company and/or Recorder's Office regarding recordation of PUD and title policy approval

EXAMPLE OF THE ITEMS THE ASSOCIATION SHOULD HAVE AT TURNOVER

These items are in addition to the items previously listed and should go back to and include all the time the developer was in control:

1. Lists of receipts and expenditures from any association funds
2. List of certificates of assessment payments, date issued and to whom
3. List of known title transfers, date and to whom
4. As_built drawings for all buildings and land
5. Original engineering drawings for all property approved by city or village
6. Original engineering specifications approved by city or village
7. Any and all specifications provided to subcontractors for work performed
8. List of all subcontractors working on project and what they did
9. Full books of account
10. Certified audit and auditor's report(s)
11. All state and/or municipal certifications
12. State and federal withholding tax receipts and FICA receipts for employees for current years
13. All bids for work to be performed

CHAPTER 3

▼

THE ANNUAL MEETING

Whether at an annual meeting of members or the initial meeting called by the developer, each year the association must elect the Board of Directors.

1. **Authority**. First, one must check the association's by_laws which establish the frequency and requirements for an election meeting. Is a mail_in ballot acceptable? Are proxies permitted? Is cumulative voting allowed? Determining these rules will underline the process of establishing procedure.

2. **Notice**. The date and timing of the notice of the meeting is set forth in the by-laws. Although Illinois courts have rules that missing a deadline by several days is not fatal to having a legal meeting, a Board must be diligent in sending out notice of the meeting in a timely fashion.

3.   **Election Procedures.** Rules of procedure should be adopted by the Board well in advance of the meeting so members are knowledgeable about qualifications. Do assessments have to be paid up? Must you be a resident to serve on the Board? Can a realtor run on behalf of an owner? Is the balloting secret or open? If the rules are established in advance, most controversies will be eliminated during the meeting. Any proxies, candidate applications and other documents that need to be sent out should be mailed in advance of any deadlines to avoid problems.

4.   **The Meeting.** If everything is prepared in advance, the meeting should go smoothly. Tally sheets, adding machines and a crew of ballot counters can dramatically reduce the meeting time.

A detailed agenda should be prepared in advance and strictly adhered to throughout the meeting. Once a quorum is established and notice is verified, introduce the chairman, announce the rules, name the candidates, accept and close nominations, and vote! Then, while the ballots are being counted, conduct the meeting. If everything runs smoothly, you can finish in an hour.

Instruct the candidates to keep their statements brief. Set time limits for questions. Do not allow the members to cross–examine the candidates. Once the ballots are counted, announce the results and prepare to adjourn the meeting. Often a Board will want to elect its officers that night. Theoretically, it should be done at a separate Board meeting, but most properties will have the balloting immediately following the election of the Board.

I am often asked whether there has to be an election when the slate of candidates is uncontested (exactly enough or less than enough candidates for the total number of vacancies). Rather than going through all of the formalities at the meeting, the chairman should entertain a motion to "accept the ballot by acclamation." Once seconded and approved by the membership by hand or voice vote, the election is complete. Collect the ballots and proxies and get on with other business. Remember, your time is valuable.

5.   **After the Meeting**. As soon as practical, the Board should meet to set goals and objectives for the year. Each new Board has its own personality. Committees should be established, rules updated, financing and budgeting procedures reviewed, etc. A veteran Board will find these tasks to be routine, whereas a brand_new Board will need considerable guidance from its professionals (manager, attorney, accountant, etc.). Remember, if you are meeting more than once a month, you are meeting too often. If your meeting lasts more than 90 minutes, it is too long. If more than a handful of owners show up every week, you are doing something wrong!

Sample Agenda for Owners'
Meeting and Election Rules
ABC CONDOMINIUM ASSOCIATION
AGENDA AND COMMENTS FOR
ANNUAL MEETING

I.   Call to order

II.   Establish notice (must be sent out not more than 30 nor less than 10 days in advance)

III.   Establish quorum (condominiums—20%; all other associations must follow by_laws)

IV.   Appoint chairman of meeting to discuss election rules (chairman of election committee, legal counsel, any other non_candidate if president is a candidate for re_election)

V.   Explain election procedures

VI.   Take nominations from the floor (if rules permit—all candidates from the floor must be nominated and seconded)

VII.   Introduce candidates (circulate biographies)

      A.   Limit remarks to two minutes

      B.   Do not allow candidates to take questions from the floor

VIII. Close nominations

IX.   Conduct final call to check in, pick up ballots and exchange proxies for ballots

X.   Appoint election monitors (must be non–candidates)

XI.   Vote

XII.   Collect ballots

XIII. Count ballots

XIV. During the counting, conduct the balance of the meeting

A. President's report—state of the association
B. Treasurer's report—financial status
C. Other reports—lawyer, accountant, engineer, etc.
D. Manager's report
E. Questions from audience to Board

XV. Announce results

XVI. Adjourn

XVII. Convene Board for special Board meeting to elect officers for _____year term

Sample Rules Regarding Election of Directors

1.   **Nomination of Candidate for the Position of Director.** Any qualified unit owner may be a candidate for the Board of Directors (Managers). In the event that a unit owner is a legal entity, such as a corporation, partnership or a trustee under a land trust, a candidate for director may be a beneficiary, an officer, partner or employee. Note, however, in the event of a dispute, candidates may be required to verify that they are qualified by exhibiting written documentation acceptable to the present Board. Since all candidates must submit Nominating Applications, THERE WILL BE NO NOMINATIONS TAKEN FROM THE FLOOR AT THE ANNUAL MEETING.

A nomination is official when made in writing to the ABC Condominium Association, c/o Property Manager, 123 Main Street, Any Town, Illinois, and received not later than Friday, _____, 19___ at 5:00 p.m.

Qualifications: In order to run for the Board of Directors, in addition to being an owner or representing an owner, the candidate or his/her principal must be a member in good standing of the association. A member in good standing shall be any member who (a) has paid all assessments and charges owed to the association by the last day of the month preceding the election and (b) does not currently have any matters pending before the Board or its duly authorized committee relating to fines, rules or covenant violations that could impair his or her ability to hold office.

2.   **Voting.** In the election of members to the Board of Directors, each voting member may cast his or her votes for each vacancy on the Board or may cumulate votes by casting votes for less than all vacancies on the Board. Voting members must cast a separate ballot for each unit represented by the particular voting member and votes are tabulated based on the percentage of ownership. Ballots are retained by the association for a period of one year.

3.   **Proxies.** An Election Committee has been/will be appointed to monitor the election. Those owners not planning to attend the Annual Meeting who would like to vote should execute a proxy.

    A.   You may designate any person to act as your proxy at the Annual Meeting, *provided that the person so designated will in fact attend the meeting.* That person will simply present the proxy to the election tellers and receive an official ballot.

    B.   You may also use the proxy as an "absentee ballot" and vote for the designated candidate(s) of your choice.

    C.   All proxies shall be retained by the association unless the proxy giver specifically requests a proxy be returned.

4.   **Election and the Casting of Ballots.** At the Annual Meeting, a ballot is issued to each unit owner or proxy. The names of all nominees as of Friday, _____, 19___ will be on the ballot. All ballots will subsequently be collected for tabulation, under supervision of the Election

Committee. If a unit owner has given his or her proxy and then appears in person at the meeting, that proxy will be automatically revoked.

5.   **Tabulation.** Following the election, the ballots and proxies will be tallied and the aggregate vote totals determined for each nominee. All candidates for office may be present during the tabulation of ballots.

6.   **Results of Election.** As soon as the results are known, the names of the individuals elected will be announced. The _____ (_) candidates receiving the highest number of votes shall be elected for a two_year term. The remaining _____ (__) shall be elected for a one_year term. The ballots, proxies, voting member designation cards and lists, and the results of the election (including the master tally sheets) will be kept for a period of one year. After the results have been announced, the Board of Directors convenes as soon as possible to elect officers for the next year.

7.   **Campaign Rules.** All campaign literature shall be signed by the proponents thereof (by name) and shall be delivered to the various unit owners in person between the hours of 9:00 a.m. and 6:30 p.m., or by mail. NO LITERATURE SHALL BE POSTED IN OR AROUND THE BUILDING.

Sample Rules Governing Secret Ballot Elections

1. All regular and special elections for directors shall be conducted by secret ballot.
2. Only the official ballot available at the election meeting shall be counted. All unauthorized forms of ballot will be voided.
3. The only identification on the ballot will be the percentage of unit ownership.
4. All proxies and/or absentee ballots must be tendered to the Nominating Committee, the property manager or the Board no later than the date so specified. Any proxies received after the deadline will be voided.
5. No forms other than those authorized by the Board of Directors will be accepted. No owner may present more than _____ proxies granting full voting power for any election.
6. Cumulative voting is/is not permitted.
7. Any owners are permitted to solicit proxies from other owners provided that:
   A. They do not create a nuisance or disrupt the peace and tranquillity of the property.
   B. They do not make any fraudulent representation or conceal material facts.
   C. They do so for a proper purpose, which is to facilitate a fair and impartial election.
   D. They use the approved forms.
8. Any owner may revoke a proxy prior to the casting of ballots.
9. Any candidate may be present during the counting of ballots.

10.   Ballots shall be retained by the Board or its agent for a period of one year.

11.   Upon written request for inspection of ballots, only the official ballot may be viewed and copied. All proxies, absentee ballots and other forms or documents identifying how owners voted shall remain confidential.

12.   The Board may designate election monitors to check in owners, collect and count ballots, verify identification, etc. Any owner or proxy holder may be requested to produce identification and/or proof of ownership or authorization to vote on behalf of any unit or unit owner(s).

Sample Agenda for a Board Meeting

I. Owners' participation (limited to ½ hour)

II. Call to order

III. Minutes of prior meeting(s) (Accept motion to waive reading. Minutes should be prepared either in draft form so that corrections can be accepted at this juncture or in final form, which should be distributed prior to the meeting.)

IV. Treasurer's Report (reveal how much money is in the bank.)

V. Attorney's Report (If present, the attorney should report on pending legal matters that can be discussed at an open meeting and field questions pertaining only to legal matters. The attorney should then be discharged, since he or she charges by the hour.)

VI. Accountant's Report (same as above)

VII. Engineer's Report (same as above)

VIII. Manager's Report (Should highlight items of significance and be in written form so it can be referred to easily. Questions can be fielded on specific items.)

IX. Committee Reports

    A. Standing committees

        1. Buildings and grounds

        2. Judiciary

        3. Maintenance

        4. Architectural control

        5. Social/recreational

    B. Special committees

        1. Finance

        2. Nominating

       3.   Rules and regulations
       4.   Other
X.   Old Business (Continue discussion of any unfinished matters from previous meeting(s).)
XI.   New Business (itemized)
XII. Good Will and Welfare (if any)
XIII. Announcements
XIV. Adjournment

CHAPTER 4

▼

ONCE YOU ARE ON THE BOARD

With a little guidance and some common sense, your job as a Board member should not have to consume all of your spare time.

Board members are considered "fiduciaries" for the members of the association. This means that the law holds you to a standard of the highest level of trust. What this means is:

- You must avoid conflicts of interest in your decision making.

- You are required to exercise sound business judgment at all times.

- You are protected from innocent mistakes in judgment and errors and omissions made in good faith. (Be certain you have directors and officers insurance.) However, you could be liable for acts of intentional misconduct, gross negligence, criminal acts or fraud.

In carrying out your duties as a director, you should become familiar with the basic rules of parliamentary procedure for Board meetings and your association's by_laws, declaration and current financial statements. You do not need to become an expert, but should understand how the association should be operating.

As a layperson/director, you need to hire a team of professionals to advise and assist the Board in carrying out the day_to_day operations of the association. This includes a manager, lawyer, accountant, maintenance company, etc. Remember, you are running a business whose primary source of revenue is other people's money.

After each annual election, the newly constituted Board should:

- Elect officers.
- Set goals for the year.
- Become familiar with the operating budget then in effect.
- Learn about the projects and contracts in place for the coming year.
- Review the existing rules and regulations.
- Become familiar with insurance coverage.
- Make sure adequate reserves are being set aside.

Although the Board should frequently communicate with its members, this does *not* mean that all owners should have unlimited access to the directors to complain. If the association has a manager, complaints should be directed to that person or company, or the complainant should be encouraged to attend a Board meeting.

Your Board meetings should be limited to addressing the business of the association as itemized in a detailed agenda prepared before the meeting. Although a designated amount of time should be set aside exclusively for owners' questions, once the meeting begins, no one should be participating but Board members who are called upon by the president. If you stick to your agenda, most meetings can be completed in 1–1/2 hours.

One way to prepare yourself for serving on the Board is to do some reading to familiarize yourself with some of the fundamentals of Board service. Becoming familiar with the essentials of the declaration, by_laws, and rules and regulations, and reading articles and books about association Boards will make your job much easier.

CHAPTER 5

▼

EXECUTIVE OR CLOSED SESSIONS

What are the proper procedures for a Board of Directors to meet in executive session? Pursuant to §18(a)(9) and §18.5(c)(4) of the Illinois Condominium Property Act, and §108.21 of the Illinois General Not For Profit Corporation Act, meetings of the Board of Directors of an association (cooperative, common interest communities and condominium associations) must be open to any owner unless the meeting is to discuss pending or probable litigation, to consider information regarding employment or dismissal of an employee, or to discuss violations of the rules and regulations or unpaid common expenses owed to the master association. It is our opinion, based upon a review of the case law, that the term "employees" also includes contractors as well.

Section 2(x) of the Illinois Condominium Property Act defines a Board meeting as any time a quorum of the

Board gathers to conduct Board business. Most association by_laws establish that a quorum of the Board is generally a majority of the Board.

Periodically, the Board of Directors of an association or cooperative wishes to meet in executive or closed session to discuss matters defined in the preceding paragraph. For example, what if the Board meets in a closed session to discuss the performance of its manager and whether the manager should be terminated. It is our opinion that the Board's act of meeting in executive session is in compliance with state law in dealing with the removal of an employee/contractor. However, under the Open Meetings requirements of both Acts, any action taken by the Board in executive session must be voted on at an open meeting of the Board of Directors and incorporated into the minutes of the open meeting.

Many Boards have a practice of holding informal Board meetings from time to time (workshops or meetings of the committee of the whole) to discuss future agendas and issues to be brought up at formal Board meetings. This can be viewed as a violation of the strict reading of the statute because a Board meeting is defined as "any gathering" of a quorum of the members of the Board of Directors.

However, in practice, this is not feasible. It is our opinion that the key words are "Board business." We view "Board business" as that which must be voted on. If no vote is forthcoming, the Board may meet informally as a "committee of the whole" prior to an open meeting to discuss the agenda for the meeting, so long as no votes are taken on Association business. This should lead to more efficient and productive Board meetings. However, Board members must remember that no issues may be voted on and all matters discussed at these "informal meetings" that are not within the exclusions as set out in §18.5(c)(4) of the Illinois Condominium Property Act must be discussed at the next open Board meeting.

Some attorneys feel that a "closed" or "executive" session must be held in conjunction with an open meeting, i.e., before, during or immediately after. Some attorneys also interpret the wording of the statute to limit closed sessions. However, we feel that upon reading the statute, the "intent" was not to impair the operation of a Board to act efficiently, but rather to correct abuses so that Boards were not voting on Board business at secret meetings.

The issue is often raised as to whether a Board, inadvertently adopting policy or making a decision in a closed session, has acted illegally. In a strict interpretation of the statute, the Board has in fact acted improperly. The intent of the open meeting sections of the Illinois Condominium Property Act and the Illinois General Not For Profit Corporation Act is to prohibit "secret" meetings and keep owners informed. On the other hand, the statute recognizes that certain matters are too delicate to handle initially at an open meeting. Therefore, all matters to be voted on, whether discussed in executive session, new, old, pending or even emergencies, must be handled at open meetings. However, the Board should keep in mind that in the event it must handle an emergency between meetings or by the same token must take action on a matter without a vote at an open meeting, several options are available.

1. Section 108.45 of the Illinois General Not For Profit Corporation Act sets forth the procedure for informal action by the Board, whereby action

can be taken when consented to in writing and signed by all of the directors.

2. Section 108.25 of the Illinois General Not For Profit Corporation Act provides that notwithstanding the notice provisions of the statute, if a director attends any meeting, that in itself constitutes a waiver of notice for the meeting unless he or she specifically attends to object to the transaction of business because the meeting is illegal.

3. Pursuant to §108.15 of the Illinois General Not For Profit Corporation Act, unless prohibited by the by_laws, directors may participate in any meeting of the Board through the use of a conference telephone or other means where all members can participate together. Participation constitutes "presence in person." This can save the Board a lot of time and provides a convenient way to meet when it is difficult to establish a quorum.

4. Lastly, and most important, when you have taken action in the past and do not approve it until a *subsequent* meeting, you can invoke the doctrine of "ratification." Substantial case law on this subject deals with corporate actions taken by individual directors, which are attributable to the corporation. So long as any action taken at an executive session or without an open meeting constitutes a legal act of the association (something it could or should do), then the Board can ratify this action at the next opportunity, i.e., regular or special meeting, and it relates back to the date in which it took effect.

A Board must be very cautious, however, to not abuse "ratification" by creating an appearance of constantly taking actions without open meetings or by acting illegally and then trying to ratify the action at an open meeting. In those instances, the individual directors could be viewed as acting outside the scope of their authority and could be liable for any damages suffered by approving an illegal act. However, as an occasional means of dealing with emergencies or irregular situations, the law provides for this procedure.

CHAPTER 6

▼

SWEETHEART CONTRACTS

When condominiums began to develop as a mainstay of the housing industry in the early 1970s, it was not uncommon to find developer_owned management companies entering into long_term agreements with developer_controlled boards of directors (commonly referred to as "sweetheart contracts").

Numerous examples of abuse were cited in case after case of condominium owners seeking relief from fraud, misrepresentation and antitrust violations.

In the case of *Luster v. Jones*, 70 Ill. App.3d 1019, 1979, a group of aggrieved homeowners sought relief from the effects of a long_term management contract entered into with Luster, Friedman & Co. Management prior to the homeowners taking over control of the Board of Directors. Although the thrust of the opinion was to deny the homeowners the relief sought for antitrust violations, the stage was set for enabling legislation to void long_term agreements entered into between developers and their subsidiaries at excessive rates, which were being inherited by new unit owner controlled boards of directors. The Illinois legislature needed to act, and on January 1, 1978, the Illinois Condominium Property Act was amended[1] to provide for the termination of these "tie_in" relationships. However, the wording of the statute was unclear as to when a contract could be properly terminated and many associations were unsuccessful litigants as a result of this lack of clarity. Thereafter, due to the proliferation of these types of situations arising in the State of Florida, and a great deal of consumer lobbying, the United States Congress enacted the Condominium and Abuse Relief Act, 15 USC §3001, et seq., Ch. 62, on October 1, 1980. Section 3607 provided that:

> (a) Any contract or portion thereof which is entered into after the effective date of the Chapter and which:
>
>> (1) provides for operation, maintenance or management of a condominium;

---

1. *P.A. 80-1118, Section 318.2(4)*: Any contract, lease or other agreement made prior to the election of a majority of the board of managers other than the developer by or on behalf of unit owners, individually or collectively, the unit owners' association or the board of managers other than the developer by association or the board of managers, which extends for a period of more than 2 years from the recording of the declaration, shall be subject to cancellation by more than ½ of the votes of the unit owners other than the developer cast at a special meeting of members called for that purpose during a period of 90 days following expiration of the 2 year period. During the 90 day period the other party to the contract, lease, or other agreement shall also have the right of cancellation.

(2) is between such unit owners or such association and the developer or an affiliate of the developer;

(3) was entered into while such association was controlled by the developer through special developer control or because the developer held a majority of votes of such association; and

(4) is for a period of more than three years, including any automatic renewal provisions which are exercisable at the sole option of the developer or an affiliate of the developer, may be terminated without penalty by such unit owner or such association.

That statute provided for a two_year period after developer control terminated whereby a vote of 2/3 of the non_developer owned units could vote to terminate the agreement upon 90 days notice.

Although most lawyers would prefer to utilize federal sanctions for this type of abuse, there was no discussion of the remedies available to terminate non_management agreements such as maintenance, laundry room leases, landscaping, etc., if they do not qualify under §3607. Section 318.2(e), et seq., of the Illinois Condominium Property Act currently reads:

(e) Any contract, lease, or other agreement made prior to the election of a majority of the board of managers other than the developer by or on behalf of unit owners, individually or collectively, the unit owners' association or the board of managers, which extends for a period of more than 2 years from the recording of the declaration, shall be subject to cancellation by more than ½ of the votes of the unit owners other than the developer cast at a special meeting of members called for that purpose during a period of 90 days following expiration of the 2 year period. At least 60 days prior to the expiration of the 2 year period, the board of managers, or, if the Board is still under developer control, then the board of managers or the developer shall send notice to every unit owner, notifying them of this provision, what contracts, leases and other agreements are affected, and the procedure for calling a meeting of the unit owners for the purpose of voting on termination of such contracts, leases or other agreements. During the 90 day period the other party to the contract, lease or other agreement shall also have the right of cancellation.

The issue of when the two years commences and the problem with associations turned over to homeowner control after two years from the recording date of the declaration has not been addressed.

The case of *S & D Service, Inc. v. 915–925 W. Schubert Condominium Assoc.* (Ill. Appellate Court, 2nd Division, April 23, 1985, #84–1035) established the proper procedure for terminating long_term leases and contracts under §18.2.

In this case, the laundry service company (S & D) entered into a lease agreement with the developer for five years. After the developer turned over control of the association to the Board elected by the homeowners, a special meeting of members was convened pursuant to §18.2 of the Act for the purpose of voting to cancel the laundry room lease.

The homeowners voted by a 67.5% majority to cancel the lease and S & D was sent the appropriate notification.

The association subsequently disconnected and removed S & D's equipment, whereby S & D responded with an action in forcible entry and detainer to place themselves back in possession of the laundry room for wrongful termination.

The Appellate Court held that when the plaintiff filed its action in forcible entry and detainer, it had no right to possession because its lease had been terminated pursuant to the implied term of the lease, which incorporates the governing law, i.e., §18.2. Further, the plaintiff's claim to a right of possession superior to the association's was held to be without merit. When plaintiff received defendant's notice of cancellation, plaintiff's right of possession expired, and, as a tenant, it had a duty to surrender possession of the leased premises. *Poppers v. Meugher.* 148 Ill. 192, 1893. There is a caveat in this case, however. The association used "self_help" to remove S & D's equipment without due process of law and opened itself up to potential exposure for a suit for damages. This case was the governing principle in Illinois for only a short time. An entire line of cases, beginning with *Keystone Service Co. v. 5040–60 N. Marine Drive*, 153 Ill. App.3d 220, 505 N.E.2d, 478, 1987 and continuing on through *Nassau Terrace Condo. Ass'n v. Silverstein*, 182 Ill. App.3d 221, 537 N.E.2d 998, 1989, essentially emasculated the power of a Board to cancel long_term laundry room leases.

The Illinois legislature has and will continue to look at better ways to eliminate abusive contract practices. However, until the statute is further clarified, it is recommended that a Board proceed cautiously.

Clearly, there are better ways for an association to proceed other than initiating its own action by wrongfully removing equipment without due process of law.

Therefore, it is recommended that the following procedures be adopted to comply with the statute and avoid
potential liability for damages:

1. Upon obtaining control of a majority of the Board
   of Directors, the unit owners, in conjunction with
   their counsel, should review all existing contracts.

2. Determine deadlines for proper notice of termination on all contracts.

3. Should any of the contracts, which extend for a
   period of "more than 2 years from the recording
   of the declaration," be viewed as unsatisfactory in
   terms of price or performance or not in the best
   interest of the association, then the Board may
   wish to terminate this relationship.

4. Notices of a special members' meeting, and then
   the meeting itself, must be convened in accordance with the notification requirements of the
   statute and the declaration.

5. At the special meeting, a referendum should be
   conducted on the issue of cancellation of the
   contract. Ballots should be in writing and votes
   must be allocated in accordance with percentage
   of ownership pursuant to §15(b) of the Act.

6. All meetings should be conducted in accordance with the by_laws, including the recording of minutes.

7. Upon obtaining the necessary majority of unit
   owners, excluding the developer's units, an agreement or lease can be canceled.

8. The Board should then send notice of cancellation
   either by certified mail or personal delivery, setting
   forth the necessary elements of compliance with

procedures mandated by statute, including the date, time and place of the members' meeting and the results of balloting.

9.   In the event the contractor disregards the notification, the Board then has recourse with an action for injunctive relief in the instance of long_term contracts, or damages.

An association must determine that the contract to be terminated is one that was contemplated by the legislature as being abusive and that the procedures followed by the Board are in strict compliance with the statute. A condominium association can then be assured that in the event of litigation, it can establish a prima facie case that will succeed, and it will not have exposure on a counterclaim for damages. All other types of associations must live with the terms of the contract unless it can be considered so abusive as to violate common law principles of fair dealing. In all cases, the procedures established in the declaration and by-laws must also be followed.

CHAPTER 7

▼

STEPS TO CONSIDER WHEN ADDRESSING DEVELOPER DEFECTS

One of the first orders of business for a new Board is to conduct an evaluation of the physical condition of the premises and determine if there are any structural defects which need to be repaired.

Most purchase agreements for new construction in a community association contain a 12-month express warranty for materials and workmanship. In addition, there is a common law implied warranty of habitability which also exists to cover latent defects for a specified period of time after discovery. Lastly, most states have a statute of limitations on these types of defects running from the date of discovery of the defect and usually a set period of time from the actual completion of construction. The purpose of this chapter is not to discuss the legal theories and supporting case law on developer warranties, but rather to provide an easy_to_follow outline of the step_by_step approach necessary for a new Board to follow when developer_caused defects create warranty problems and homeowner complaints. Obviously, emergencies need to be addressed at once.

1. **Determining the Scope and Extent of the Defects**

New construction requires a "breaking_in" period involving building settlement, seasoning of wolmanized lumber, concrete drying, etc. The hardest thing for a newly elected Board of Directors to determine is, when is it the appropriate time to initiate a comprehensive physical inspection of the premises. Statute of limitations permitting, it is recommended that an association experience a full cycle of seasons prior to commencing the final inspection process. Serious defects apparent to the untrained eye should obviously be handled on an ongoing basis and members should be reminded to report defects promptly.

2. **The Spring Walk_Through**

In the first Spring following a cycle of seasons, a committee should be designated to walk the grounds and inspect the premises to make note of obvious physical defects. Chipping paint, cracked masonry, dead shrubbery, etc., should be specifically identified by location. Often a builder will request to participate in a walk_through to create its own list of "things to do."

3. **How to Assess the Damages**

Since an association Board of Directors generally consists of lay people, an association, regardless of size, should retain the services of a qualified and licensed architectural/engineering firm. After drawing up specifications, soliciting competitive bids and carefully checking references, the Board should select an expert that (a) is experienced in dealing with multifamily residential development and (b) is an acceptable candidate for maintaining a long_term relationship with the Board.

Once retained, the engineer should be given the Board's inspection report and any homeowner complaints and service requests as a starting point. The engineer will then need to compile a comprehensive report containing the following information:

- Scope, extent and location of defects
- Building code violations (if any)
- Cause of defects
- Recommended procedures for curing the defects
- Itemized costs for any repairs to be made
- Anticipated remaining useful life of all major amenities (roofs, parking lots, siding, etc.)

The purpose of the comprehensive report is three_fold: (1) to establish a basis for discussions with the developer for possible settlement in instances of developer liability, (2) to establish an initial evidentiary basis for potential litigation, and probably most important, (3) to provide the Board of Directors with sufficient information to establish long_term contingency reserves by allocating an appropriate percentage of future assessment revenues to long_term maintenance projects. The Illinois Condominium Property Act suggests that such a "reserve" study is almost imperative.

4.   Commencing Negotiations

Once the engineering report has been completed, the developer should be notified in writing as to the extent and scope of the defects and should be invited to meet informally to discuss the issues. It is recommended that the association be prepared to provide a copy of the engineering report to the developer for purpose of analysis and discussion by the developer's staff. Efforts at accommodation, conciliation and negotiation must be exhausted prior to considering litigation.

If a developer is willing to meet to discuss the issues, an association should be prepared to refute the customary defenses of:

- Ordinary wear and tear not covered by warranty
- Lack of preventive maintenance
- Negligence
- Waiver of the implied warranty in the purchase agreement

Once negotiations commence, the question of whether the developer should be permitted to return to the property to make repairs often arises. It is my opinion that the case law requires that a builder be given a reasonable opportunity to cure construction defects. A Board must always demonstrate an ability to be reasonable. However, this must be dictated by the specific circumstances. The Board must consider whether: (a) this particular developer has a track record for living up to his word; (b) this is merely a stall tactic or (c) the repair work will be as bad as or worse than the original construction.

In most instances, the developer should be given a reasonable opportunity to return to the premises to attempt to repair defects up to a certain point. Since the statute of limitations is fixed from the point of discovery and arguably begins with the completion of the engineering study, the developer should be permitted to continue repair work unless it jeopardizes the association's legal position. As a practical matter, many developers are savvy enough to build into the purchase price of the unit a percentage of their profit to be used for settlement proceeds that will then be given back to the association for repair work in exchange for a final release. Lastly, any remedial repairs should be monitored and inspected by the association's engineer to assure a high quality of performance.

5.   **When Negotiation Is Unsuccessful**

When the developer is unwilling to commence or continue substantive negotiations, the Board of Directors must make an initial determination whether the defects are substantial enough to warrant legal action. In conjunction with the association's attorney and engineer, a determination must be made whether legal and engineering fees and costs can justify the costs of a lawsuit. An estimate of costs and fees will provide evidence of whether the suit is economically feasible, since it is unlikely that legal and engineering fees are recoverable. The Board should also obtain a legal opinion as to the legal theories of recovery and the risks and liability involved in pursuing litigation.

Once all the information has been properly evaluated, it should then be brought to the attention of the members of the association.

6.   **Advising the Membership**

Although the final decision to sue a developer lies within the discretion of the Board of Directors, it would be a critical error in judgment for a Board to consider such a move in a vacuum. Due to the potential for enormous costs and lengthy delay, the Board must remember that it will be the members who are going to underwrite these expenses for a considerable period of time.

An open meeting of the members should be called to meet with the Board, legal counsel and engineer. The engineering report should be summarized, costs and risks of litigation must be explained and an opportunity for homeowners to ask questions is essential.

An advisory, non_binding referendum should be conducted to provide the Board with the advice and consent of the members. Although it is ultimately up to the Board to vote on the final decision, it would not be prudent to approve an action of such magnitude contrary to the wishes of a substantial majority of the members.

After several years of litigation, new Boards may question the judgment of those previous directors who voted to initiate litigation. All they see are costs being expended for lawyers, engineers and repairs and nothing in return. The old Board members and the lawyer are blamed, and there is a tendency to push for a quick settlement for far less than the case is worth.

7. **Final Resolution**

The downside of the lawsuit is the three to seven years of potential intense litigation, deteriorating buildings, enormous costs, depreciating property values, directors' time off from work to give depositions and testify at trial, the possibility of appeal and possibly an insolvent developer waiting at the end. In most instances these cases settle at some point in the litigation. Before running "head on" into aggressive defense counsel, the Board must look at all of the costs and risks and examine its decision_making process very carefully. The Board may have to decide that once it is past the nasty letter stage, it would be better off setting up sufficient reserves to do the repairs on an ongoing basis and forego the suit entirely.

In conclusion, a Board must weigh all of the factors that go into a "final declaration of war." If negotiations are proceeding positively, the Board must have an effective negotiator acting on its behalf (who may not have the same personality and approach as a tenacious litigator who will try the case). It is far more productive to spend six to 18 months in substantive negotiations if a fair settlement is foreseeable. Most importantly, the Board must be firm in resisting pressure to jump into a lawsuit which will cost more to pursue than what can be recovered in the best case scenario. An association can only recover damages that it can legitimately prove and the costs of repair must justify the costs of litigation. However, once decided on, the lawsuit should be pursued aggressively until it is resolved successfully, by trial or settlement.

CHAPTER 8

▼

SELECTING CONTRACTORS

According to the governing documents, the Board of Directors is responsible for administering and maintaining the property. The Illinois Condominium Property Act states that the "unit owner's association is responsible for the overall administration of the property through its duly elected board of managers." Often, the Board retains or employs a wide variety of professionals and contractors to accomplish those tasks.

The by_laws should spell out in detail the Board's authority to engage a management company and establish the obligation for maintenance, repair and replacement of the common areas. Most associations require the services of either on_site employees or outside professionals and contractors to provide the services needed to fulfill these obligations. For employees, the Board should have an agreement spelling out the job description and specific duties, as well as all compensation, benefits and termination. The Board also must establish a procedure to follow when outside services are required. Most often, the property manager contacts the potential contractors to submit their credentials and a bid for the Board's consideration.

Development of Specifications

A detailed description of the services to be rendered must be developed. These "specifications" will form the basis for the contractual arrangement between the association and the contractor. All specifications should identify the insurance requirements expected of the contractor and the time frame for beginning and finishing the project. The amount of detail in the specifications will depend on the nature of the service or project. Specifications for engineering or management services generally are more detailed than those for other professional services. Landscaping, maintenance and repair projects often require very detailed specifications and periodic supervision.

What is most important is that potential bidders base their price on uniform requirements. The Board, in comparing various contract proposals, must be able to differentiate between "apples and apples." Remember, never let the contractor, who has an economic interest in the job itself, develop the specifications. An engineer, architect or specialist should be consulted to develop the job standards before bids are sought.

After specifications are developed, they are presented to the Board for discussion and approval and then the job is put out for bid. The proposal should state when a response is due and to whom it must be submitted. There is no specific legal requirement as to how many bids should be sought, but a minimum of three is customary. Bids do not have to be sealed, but it is recommended to maintain confidentiality.

Evaluation of Proposals

The Board then reviews the recommendations from a committee or the proposals themselves. After careful consideration of the various aspects of each proposal and comparison of the proposals, the Board selects the contractor at an open meeting.

Preparation of the Contract

Legal counsel should then be consulted for review or preparation of the contract. The specifications generally are made part of the agreement. The contract must identify the parties, the obligations of each party, payment terms and conditions, termination and default provisions, notice and insurance requirements. After discussions with the contractor and finalization of the agreement, the Board authorizes the president of the association to sign the document on behalf of the association. By signing the contract, the parties indicate their acceptance of the terms and agree to abide by them. Remember, if you try to save legal fees by not having an attorney review the agreement, you run the risk that it may cost many thousands of dollars to resolve a dispute that was not addressed in the agreement.During performance of the contract, a designated individual, usually the property manager, is charged with supervisory responsibility. On a large job, such as a roof, an architect or roofing consultant should be engaged to inspect the job and approve payouts on an ongoing basis.

Payment must be approved by the Board in accordance with bill_paying procedures. Payments should be made as required by the contract, unless a dispute over the contractor's performance arises. Discussions about any problems should commence with the intention of resolving the matter swiftly. When a bank loan is involved, often payments will be generated from an escrow account after each inspection and approval. Remember, *always* get waivers of lien for each contractor, subcontractor and material supplier prior to tendering payment.

Contracts with Board members or with companies in which Board members have an interest must be fully disclosed to the membership in advance of the Board's vote. Those arrangements should be scrutinized very closely, and of course, the Board member must abstain from voting on any issue where he or she has an economic interest. Section 18(a) of the Illinois Condominium Property Act requires that directors who have an interest in any business that contracts with the association must be fully disclosed to the membership. Procedures have been established to allow members to petition the Board to overturn the agreement.

Conclusion

The Board of Directors must follow its procedures consistently. In this way, the Board can fulfill its fiduciary duty to the members and protect itself from liability. Proper procedures can and do lead to good contracts and minimize disputes and unnecessary litigation.

CHAPTER 9

▼

ADOPTING A BUDGET

Each common interest community, whether it is a cooperative, condominium, master, homeowners, townhome or other entity, is required to develop an annual operating budget and establish or follow the procedures set forth in the association's by_laws. Sometimes an association's financial condition requires a mid_year adjustment in the form of a supplemental budget or even a special assessment. The by_laws should outline the proper procedure.

Condominium Associations

A condominium association's Board of Directors must "prepare and distribute to all unit owners a detailed proposed annual budget, setting forth with particularity all anticipated common expenses by category, as well as all anticipated assessments and other income." [Illinois Condominium Property Act, §9(c)] The total amount of anticipated expenses must be calculated using the previous year's history, inflation, contract escalation clauses, increased expenses, etc. Each owner's proportionate share of the expenses is then calculated based on his or her percentage of ownership. Once the amount is determined, it is divided by the installments (usually 12) and each owner receives a notice of his or her obligation for the next year.

Sections 18.4(b), (c) and (d) of the Illinois Condominium Property Act grant the Board of Managers (Directors) the exclusive power to prepare, adopt and distribute the annual budget for the property, to levy the assessments and to collect assessments from the unit owners, provided it stays within certain guidelines. In the event an annual operating budget exceeds 115% of the previous year's collections (assessments, special assessments, etc.), then a petition filed with the Board by 20% of the homeowners can force a meeting so that the owners can review this decision [§18(a)(8)]. Also, the Act requires certain provisions be included in the association's by_laws to implement those powers and duties.

Each unit owner must receive, at least 30 days prior to adoption by the Board of Directors, a copy of the proposed annual budget together with an indication of which portions are non_recurring expenses or what amounts are being set aside for reserves. All budgets adopted after July 1, 1990 require that reasonable reserves be provided for capital expenditures and deferred maintenance [§9(a)(2)] unless the association opts out (see next chapter).

Each year the Board, with the assistance of its manager, should prepare and review a pro_forma budget to be submitted to its members. Between checking the expenditures on the previous year's financial statements and communicating with contractors and materials and service providers regarding the coming year's prices, the Board should have sufficient data with which to draft a budget. A prudent association will begin this process at the end of the third quarter of its fiscal or calendar year. Self_managed properties should obtain input from their accountant.

Ideally, a finance committee should do the initial review before it is submitted to the Board. However, many associations are unable to solicit enough volunteers for a committee and the Board does all of the work.

Once the numbers are reworked to a reasonable level, taking into account price increases, contingent liabilities, reserves, deferred maintenance, etc., a proposed budget must be sent out to the members either in accordance with the by_laws or 30 days prior to adoption, if it is an Illinois condominium.

After the homeowners have provided input at a meeting, the Board can then adopt the budget in accordance with prescribed procedures.

All Other Associations

Umbrella or Master Associations. Section 18.5 of the Illinois Condominium Property Act establishes identical procedures for master associations as are required of condominium associations.

Cooperatives, Townhome or Homeowners Associations. The Board of Directors of a townhome or homeowners association or a cooperative must conduct itself in compliance with the association's declaration, articles of incorporation, by_laws and §101.01–117.20 of the Illinois General Not For Profit Corporation Act, if it is incorporated. The procedures for adopting the budget and allocating the assessments should be set forth in the by_laws. Although most associations and cooperatives require that the Board adopt the budget, by_laws do sometimes contain member approval requirements.

Cooperatives are governed by either corporate by_laws or a trust agreement, depending on the format under which they operate.

Supplemental Budgets and Special Assessments. Where operating capital is insufficient and a deficit is looming, most by_laws permit the Board to propose a re_vamped budget to be sent out mid_year. The procedures are generally different for each association, although they usually mirror the rules governing the annual operating budget. When a specific project requires capital that is non_existent, the association can also levy a special assessment in accordance with the by_laws. Section 18(a)(8) of the Illinois Condominium Property Act sets out the procedures for condominiums.

The 1994 amendments to the Illinois Condominium Property Act give the Board great latitude in handling emergencies—virtually unlimited authority. However, all other special assessments can be limited by the owners, who can force a referendum.

Association documents also deal with the issue of surplus funds collected during the fiscal year in excess of the actual expenditures for the year. A refund to the owners or application of the surplus to future assessment payments is often referred to. However, the Board should amend the budget and allocate the surplus funds to specified reserve accounts. This should also protect the association from any claim by the Internal Revenue Service that the surplus funds are income and subject to federal taxation and eliminate the need to refund surplus funds. Recently the IRS has begun to attack this exemption in other states. The accountant should advise the association on the best course of action.

It is always important for a Board to explore ways to raise cash in the event of a shortfall. A non_cooperative homeowners group can create havoc if it does not cooperate with the Board on a supplemental assessment. Although a bank loan can be procured as a stop_gap, it is important for the by_laws to give the Board the necessary latitude to raise money.

Ongoing Review. The budget committee's job is really not over, even after the budget has been adopted. In conjunction with the association's treasurer, each month the operating statement should be reviewed thoroughly to make sure that the budget is realistic and does not require an interim adjustment.

CHAPTER 10

▼

RESERVE OR BORROW:
CAPITAL EXPENDITURES AND
DEFERRED MAINTENANCE

At some point in the life of an association, the Board will be confronted with the problem of how to pay for a major repair program. Special assessment powers are established by statute and/or in the governing documents which usually give the Board sufficient authority to raise the necessary funds to cover the cost of the repair(s).

However, large special assessments can create a financial hardship for the individual owners and sometimes provisions in the by_laws setting "caps" requiring homeowner approval can limit the Board's ability to contract for the entire repair program.

The Illinois Condominium Property Act was amended in 1990 to impose reserve requirements on condominium associations (§9); the philosophy behind this statutory mandate was to compel Boards to commence "forced" savings plans in order to reduce the need for frequent or large special assessments. The Act sets forth the following criteria for a Board to consider when preparing an annual operating budget:

- Repair and replacement costs and the estimated useful life of the property
- The current and anticipated return on association funds
- Any independent professional reserve study which the association may obtain
- The financial impact on unit owners and on the market value of the condominium units of any assessment increase needed to fund reserves
- The ability of the association to obtain funding

If the declaration does not impose reserve requirements, two_thirds of the owners can vote to opt out of the requirement to maintain reserves.

However, even if an association keeps reserves to a minimum under one of the above scenarios, or opts out, it could be creating an unforeseen problem for its members in chilling resales and refinancing. Mortgage lenders now look at an association's financial statement before approving a loan and an underfunded reserve could quash the ability of unit owners to obtain financing or sell their unit.

In the event the association's reserve accounts are underfunded or the owners have voted to opt out, the Board is left with the third alternative—financing the project. Section 18.4(m) of the Illinois Condominium

Property Act permits associations to borrow money if it is not prohibited in the declaration or by_laws. All other types of associations can rely on their documents or §103.10 of the Illinois General Not For Profit Corporation Act for their grant of authority.

In applying for a loan, the association and the lender must consider the following issues:

- Source of authority to borrow funds
- Making the debt service affordable
- No pre–payment penalties
- Borrowing only as much as is needed (A line of credit is preferable to a fixed amount, since some members may opt to pre_pay their share, which would entail borrowing less money.)
- Collateral—the association cannot pledge the dwelling units, since only an individual can do that. A cooperative can mortgage a building, but a condominium or homeowners association does not have that authority. An association can mortgage separately held common areas, i.e., club-house, recreational facility, etc., and it can pledge accounts receivable. An association can also grant certain rights in the event of a default, such as the right of the lender to record liens and fore-close on units in the event of a default.
- Loan documents must be tailor_made to association needs without granting the lender unreasonable levels of power.

In negotiating a loan, it is important for the Board to have the advice of counsel, particularly since most loan packets require a legal opinion contingent upon review of all of the loan documents.

Although the chances of an association defaulting on a loan are minimal, in the event this should happen, the Board should have a contingency plan to avoid a multiple foreclosure action being filed against all owners. Because association loans have such a low potential for default, many contractors will do their own financing.

The biggest risk for an association is a reduced payment loan arrangement with a balloon payment at the end. In the event the association is unable to pay off the balloon in a lump sum, or refinance, it could be facing a default. Therefore, it is always wise to amortize the entire loan balance over a fixed period of time to assure repayment.

In conclusion, to raise the necessary cash to underwrite a major project, the association can opt for:

- Special assessment;
- Transfer money from reserves; or
- Financing.

What works best for one association may not work for another and an association can use a hybrid approach to combine all three options. This would cushion the adverse impact on the association's financial statement.

CHAPTER 11

▼

RECOMMENDED PROCEDURES FOR KEEPINGMINUTES FOR PROPERTY OWNERS' ASSOCIATIONS

In Illinois, all condominium associations are deemed to have all of the powers of a not_for_profit corporation, whether or not they have actually incorporated. As a matter of policy, most common interest communities, including both co_ops and condominiums, are incorporated as not_for_profit corporations and, therefore, governed by the General Not For Profit Corporation Act. (Some co_ops are established as Trusts.)

In all instances, the Board of Directors is required to keep minutes of its regular and special meetings. The minutes of a meeting are the official summary of all business that was transacted. However, a frequent area of dispute is whether the minutes contain sufficient detail or whether the recording secretary should note every item of business discussed at the meeting.

An association, or any corporation for that matter, keeps minutes to preserve a permanent record of all action(s) taken at the meetings of the directors and/or the members. A Board speaks through its records, and the minutes are a definitive part of that record. Also, to avoid misunderstandings which may occur in the event of litigation, accurate records serve as a guideline for directors in carrying out their decisions.

In general, there is a legal presumption that the official minutes of a corporation cover the entire subject or transaction recorded, even if the records prove to be incomplete or ambiguous. In those areas where there is a discrepancy, a court of law may permit other evidence to be submitted, including oral testimony to contradict an incomplete statement.

The by_laws of an association are intended to provide the operating rules for the corporation. Generally they may provide that the secretary of the corporation act as the secretary of a meeting of all directors or members. However, the association can retain the services of an outside party to do the actual recording, and then the secretary of the corporation need only certify the accuracy of the minutes. Regardless, the recorder of the proceedings should take careful notes of all discussions that take place and all actions taken, so that the minutes constitute an accurate and full report of the proceedings. Minutes should be recorded in clear and concise language; they must be complete and accurate. All matters of importance should be noted, simply and unambiguously.

The secretary should keep in mind that the directors stand in a fiduciary relationship to the members of the association. This requires them to exercise the utmost good faith and due diligence. Courts have recently held that a resolution adopted by the Board of Directors constitutes a contract between the Board and the membership. A Board can then be accused of violating this contract with its membership if proper records are not maintained. The following guidelines illustrate the proper procedure for taking minutes.

1. The president, or someone with delegated authority, should prepare a written agenda for the meeting. This allows everyone in attendance to follow the matters at hand and also allows the recording secretary to prepare in advance for each item of business to be discussed. A statement is then noted in advance of the discussion of each matter on the agenda which is about to be discussed. No attempt should be made to put everything down in full. Occasionally a comment may be inserted which may explain a statement made or a decision arrived at.

2. Arguments on particular questions and discussions that take place are not made a part of the record unless a member of the Board specifically requests that his or her view be made a matter of record. However, a summary of an opinion will suffice as opposed to a verbatim recital of the entire statement. Remember, this is not the Congressional Record.

3. It is sometimes advisable to include a statement explaining a resolution or motion to clarify a proposal.

4. Sometimes written resolutions should be drafted in advance by legal counsel in order to clarify a certain subject matter or where legal technicalities are involved.

5. The name(s) of proponents and seconders of motions are generally omitted, although in some cases it may be advisable if the matter is of significant importance or highly controversial. This is left to the recorder's discretion.

6. It is not necessary to record the names of those voting for or against a routine proposition. Only in matters of great importance should the names of those voting in favor of or contrary to the resolution be recorded, if there is a roll-call vote.

7. Where a special request is made for recording a dissenting vote by a minority, such entry should be carefully noted in the record. It is also important to note any director who is personally or financially interested in a particular transaction and did not vote as a result of a conflict of interest or is not present. All conflicts of interest must be fully disclosed. The Illinois Condominium Property Act requires all condominium directors to discuss economic conflicts to the membership.

8. If no vote is taken, it is sufficient to note in the minutes that "it was the consensus that" or "each director present expressed his or her approval of" or that "doubt was expressed as to," followed by a statement of facts.

In summary, minutes usually begin with a statement as to the time and place of the meeting, establish that the meeting was properly called and that proper notice was given, include the names of the chairman and those present, and give an indication that there was a quorum. The minutes should then state that the minutes of the previous meeting were presented, and then a clear, accurate and complete report of all the business transacted should be included in accordance with the established order of business of that meeting, including the ultimate motion to adjourn.Also, complete minutes are important to maintain rules and regulations. It is recommended that the Board or the rules committee of an association update the rules and regulations on an annual basis, by reviewing the previous year's minutes and resolutions in order to incorporate all new or revised policies into the operating documents. Since the rules and regulations are a "living, breathing" document governing day_to_day living, they must be maintained to reflect all changes of policy.

Finally, with regard to approval of the minutes, for purposes of clarification and time economy, a copy of the minutes should be sent to Board members in advance of each meeting so that they may be reviewed before the meeting in which they are to be approved. It is recommended that a motion be made to waive the reading of the minutes and that any corrections or additions be made of record, followed by the preparation of a statement of corrections to be incorporated in the corporate records of the association. Minutes and other written reports should not be read verbatim, as they speak for themselves. Any director who has dissented on any business from a prior meeting who believes that any order of business is not in the best interests of the association should carefully examine the minutes in order to note that this dissent was entered. Otherwise, a mere summary of the business and transactions of the association should be adequate for reflecting the corporation business. A motion should then be adopted to approve the minutes as corrected (if applicable) or approved as read, and the minutes should be adopted.

In conclusion, the minutes of the association are the permanent record of all corporate transactions and business of the Board. They should reflect the specific motions and resolutions that have been adopted and any significant discussion should be summarized as well. However, minutes should not be a verbatim recitation of the discussions, arguments, conclusions, opinions, etc., of the members of the Board of Directors or members of the association, as this creates confusion and could possibly generate additional liability in the event of litigation. As previously stated, it is best to make a clear, concise summary and a definitive statement as to the specific business and record the votes only where absolutely necessary.

By following this procedure, the Board can reduce the length of its meetings, prepare a professional document, limit its liability and maintain a permanent record of proceedings to guide future Boards.

CHAPTER 12

▼

ADOPTING RULES AND REGULATIONS

The Operating Documents

From its inception, each cooperative, condominium and homeowners association derives its powers from a set of initial operating documents, usually in the form of a declaration of covenants and a set of by_laws, and by statute.

The declarations (whether condominium ownership or covenants, conditions and restrictions of record) are the recorded covenants which run with the land and govern the administration and maintenance of the entire property. The covenants usually set forth the guidelines for association versus unit owner responsibilities, permissible or proscribed activities, insurance requirements, budgeting and assessment procedures, etc.

The by_laws are the operating document for the corporate structure itself. They are generally separate and apart from the declaration (although sometimes wrongfully incorporated). The by_laws establish the Board of Directors, when and how it is to be elected, the functions it serves, when and where it meets, etc.

The by_laws are usually recorded at the time the not_for_profit corporation is established with the state. The amendment process requires that amendments to the declaration and sometimes the by_laws be approved by a "super" majority of the association membership (including co-ops) and re_recorded before they take effect (two_thirds, three_fourths, etc.).

However, the typical declaration and by_laws are generally deficient in providing specific information about the requirements of day_to_day living at the property. Furthermore, since the declaration and by_laws usually require a two_thirds or three_fourths majority to approve any amendments, it is not practical to incorporate laundry room hours, garbage pickups, pool rules, etc., when modifications are so difficult and cumbersome to achieve. Therefore, most governing documents and in some instances statutory authority (e.g., §18.4 *et seq.* of the Illinois Condominium Property Act) authorize the Board of Directors to adopt reasonable rules and regulations.

The rules and regulations are a significant source of authority for the Board because they are the "living and breathing" document that governs the day_to_day operations of any association. The rules and regulations should read between the lines of the declaration and by_laws and have the same force and effect as a municipal ordinance for a municipality, which is also governed by the constitution, as well as statutes, of the federal, state and local authorities.

Although a developer may use an identical set of declarations and by_laws for more than one property, this cannot be said for rules and regulations, since no two developments are alike in the way they are administered.

Initial Drafting

Once a Board is elected and controlled by the membership, one of its very first tasks should be the adoption of the initial set of rules and regulations.

First, the Board should create a special committee comprised of one Board member and several interested homeowners. The committee's sole purpose should be to create an initial draft for full Board review.

Second, it is a good idea to obtain sample copies of rules and regulations from other similarly situated associations to use as examples. Then, specific guidelines can be established which are peculiar to particular needs, but at least there is a framework to follow without "re_inventing the wheel." Also, some of the more relevant portions of the declaration and by_laws should be included by removing the "legalese" and rewording these provisions in plain English.

Third, all categories and specific rules should be numbered for future reference.

Finally, once an acceptable draft is agreed on by the committee, it should be submitted to the association's legal counsel for a legal review. This will allow the attorney the opportunity to make sure that the proposed rules and regulations conform to the governing documents and statutes and contain no illegal provisions.

Thereafter, the preliminary draft is submitted to the Board of Directors for its review and the preparation of a final draft.

Adoption

The final draft should then be sent to all members of the association in conjunction with a notice of a special meeting of the association to discuss the rules and regulations. (For condominiums in Illinois, this is mandatory under §18.4, *et seq.,* of the Illinois Condominium Property Act.)

This special meeting allows homeowners an opportunity to give their input and ask questions. However, the ultimate authority to adopt the rules and regulations lies exclusively with the Board, as the elected representatives of the association.

The "final/final" draft, which becomes the official operating document, should then be ratified at the next regular or special meeting of the Board of Directors. The document should be in the possession of all owners and renters, as well as all future residents.

Operation

The rules and regulations of an association are only as good as the efforts of the Board to enforce them. This requires the education of all present and future residents as to their stipulations, as well as the procedures for enforcement, such as fines and legal action. Copies should be made readily available at a nominal charge and all new residents, whether tenants or owners, must receive a current copy and should acknowledge receipt in writing to be kept on file by the association.Pertinent sections should be reproduced and posted at the appropriate places on the property (pool rules at the pool, laundry rules in the laundry rooms, etc.).

Finally, members of the association must be constantly reminded that the elected Board of Directors and the manager are not the local police department and cannot be expected to witness all violations and solve all disputes between residents. The members of the association must be willing to come forward and notify the

Board or file complaints when rule violations occur.
They must also be willing to give testimony to prove the
accusations in order for the Board to utilize prescribed
enforcement procedures.

Violations of the law, however, must be reported to the
police, and, as a practical matter, the association should
refrain from getting involved in simple "neighbor" disputes that do not affect the common areas or the health,
safety and welfare of the members of the association.

Enforcement

The association must have a specific, detailed procedure for enforcing punishment of rule infractions.
Whether it is arbitration proceedings, denial of privileges,
fines, etc., the procedure must be set forth in precise
detail. Paramount to imposition of any punishment is
"Notice" and an "opportunity to be heard." (§18.4(e)
Illinois Condominium Property Act) Once an association
assumes police powers, it must afford the accused due
process. By offering all accused rule violators an opportunity for a fair and impartial hearing, an association can
avoid being accused of being "arbitrary and capricious."

It is recommended that a separate committee be cho-
sen for hearing rule violation proceedings, with the Board
being the final arbiter. After notice is sent and a hearing is
held (with or without the accused being present), the
committee should then deliberate in private. The committee's recommendation should be submitted to the
Board to be voted on at the next open meeting.
Thereafter, a written finding should be sent to the
accused. In this way, the Board remains detached from
the hearing process and maintains its objectivity in the
event of a request for reconsideration. Disputes between

owners can be arbitrated or mediated. The enforcement procedure should also specify a schedule of fines, suspension of privileges, legal remedies and other details, including an admonishment that the guilty party will be responsible for the association's costs and legal fees in the event legal proceedings are warranted.

Remember, a Board member cannot vote or even sit on the reviewing tribunal if he or she is a complaining witness or an accused.

Periodic Review and Update

For rules and regulations to be truly effective, they must be kept up to date. It is recommended that each year the Rules Committee be reconvened to review the existing documents, copies of minutes of the previous year's Board meetings and copies of all amendments, resolutions, motions and changes in the law. Any changes or additions should be incorporated in order to update the rules and regulations on an ongoing and regularly scheduled basis. It is further recommended that an association forego the expensive printing and utilize a flexible and economical method of reproducing the Rules so that an annual revision or re_duplication is not a major financial burden.

Copies of changes and modifications should be sent to all members of the association without the necessity of a meeting, unless the entire set is being substantially revised.

Complete copies of the revised rules and regulations should be given to all new and existing residents upon request. The Board can charge a reasonable fee (§19 Illinois Condominium Property Act) for production costs and administration.

By establishing a tradition of having an annual review, the rules and regulations will not get stale and the association can avoid having a rule struck down by a court for arbitrary enforcement of rules governing inapplicable situations. By implementing a policy of annual review, the Board of Directors also satisfies some potential concerns of its Errors and Omissions insurance carrier.

A recent trend in the courthouse is that judges will often look at the specificity and detail contained in the rules, as well as notice to all residents, before deciding the outcome of any case involving enforcement. It is obviously in the association's best interest to have a well_drafted set of rules.

CHAPTER 13

▼

RISKS AND LIABILITIES FOR PROPERTY MANAGERS

In administering the affairs of an association, the manager is often required to consult with an attorney, insurance broker, accountant and other professionals to properly advise a Board on how to manage risk potential and reduce exposure for a myriad of liabilities. Yet, how many property management companies turn this focus inward to reduce their own legal risks and liabilities? A property management company must also look carefully at its structure and office operations to make sure that the controls that it is recommending to its clients also are being applied internally. There are a number of potential "trouble spots" and a simple audit of these areas can minimize a property management company's exposure to unnecessary liability.

Selecting and Maintaining the Business Entity

Initially, a management company must select the appropriate business format. If it is a sole proprietorship, the manager must consider aspects of personal liability, the tax considerations, the variations on retirement and employee benefit requirements and possible limitations on available insurance. A partnership incurs the same risks and spreads it among two or more people.

A major consideration for individuals and partners is personal responsibility for management company debts and activities. Incorporating a management company shields the personal assets of the principal(s) from the creditors and potential plaintiffs. Limited liability corporations in Illinois give property managers an additional level of protection.

Maintaining a corporate "veil" can protect a manager's personal assets and estate from most creditors and most forms of liability. It is not totally "sue_proof," nor does it shield acts of dishonesty, but the prudent manager can implement procedures to limit exposure.

Corporations acting in their own name are deemed "fictional persons" under the law and obligations that are taken on by the corporation (and not personally guaranteed by any individual) will shield the officers, directors and shareholders of the corporation from personal liability. For a nominal fee and by filing papers annually, the owners of the corporation can be insulated from liability for negligence, personal injury and property damage not covered by insurance.

Certain preventive measures must be taken to secure these protections. Managers must always be acting within the scope of their authority. They must always disclose their relationship with the corporation (president, director, etc.) when signing documents. Corporate activities must be those that are reasonably contemplated in the ordinary course of business.

The corporate format must be maintained on an ongoing basis, i.e., holding meetings when required, obtaining appropriate waivers of notice of meeting, preparing necessary governmental forms, keeping minutes current, adopting resolutions and amending corporate documents when necessary.

Limiting Liability

The owners of the management company must make sure that they and their employees are at all times acting within the scope of their authority. Activities must be limited to those reasonably contemplated by the business entity and those which are required to be performed within the scope of any written agreement.

For example, receiving referral fees (or kickbacks) from association contractors could expose a manager to personal liability. Additionally, a manager who signs a contract without authorization could incur unexpected financial liability.

In order to minimize the adverse effects of accidental loss, the management company must maintain comprehensive insurance coverage, i.e., personal injury, property damage, premises liability, errors and omissions, worker's compensation, etc.

Notwithstanding the fact that a management company is generally protected from many areas of liability by provisions contained in its agreement with a client, there are many instances when this alone is not sufficient. In most personal injury or property damage actions against an association, the manager will often be named as a party and sometimes the manager is defended through the property's insurance coverage under a reservation of rights. This allows the insurance carrier to defend the case, but reserve its rights under the policy to deny coverage for any verdict under certain circumstances. That is why it is critical for the management company to have its own comprehensive insurance coverage in the event the association's carrier ultimately denies coverage.

Management companies are often named as defendants in slip and fall cases, car accidents on the property, leaky roofs, wrongful evictions, retaliatory actions for car towing, etc. As stated above, it is important for the property manager to check the association's insurance coverage to make sure he or she is covered under all contingencies. If the property manager is an employee, the association must maintain worker's compensation protection. For management companies, they could have their own policy in place.

Considering that the bulk of association directors and officers insurance and liability coverage premiums go to the cost of defense, a manager should have the benefit of an insurance company paid attorney, rather than having to spend its own funds on legal counsel. Some insurance policies for associations have provisions that allow the insured to select its own counsel, subject to approval by the carrier. This allows the manager/association to select the firm it is familiar with as long as the carrier grants final approval.

Non_Covered Risks

Intentional acts and civil rights violations are often not covered by any type of insurance. Although bonding can be put in place to protect against losses from employee/manager dishonesty, there is no coverage for a "punch in the nose."

Also, discriminatory policies in leasing or rule enforcement can also take a manager, as well as a Board, outside the scope of insurance coverage.

This is why it is important for a property manager to be cautious in handling Board business as well as counseling the Board as its designated professional. When a Board refuses to heed prudent advice and enlarges its exposure to a possible lawsuit, the manager must document in writing that: (a) he or she advised against this action; (b) the Board disregarded the manager's recommendation and (c) he or she is not responsible for any of the consequences as a result of the Board's actions (C.Y.A.).

Conclusion

The most important consideration in operating a management business is to follow the same advice you should be giving to your clients. Use "sound business judgment" in all decision making, check with legal counsel when a decision has to be made that involves some type of risk, have your accountant review your internal procedures periodically and make sure your insurance coverage is comprehensive, up_to_date and has adequate policy limits.

By following this simple game plan, a management company can concentrate its efforts on the more significant issues of controlling its own overhead, marketing, diversifying its activities(rentals, maintenance, sales, etc.), expanding its client base and, of course, making a profit.

CHAPTER 14

▼

INSURANCE

The Illinois Condominium Property Act and the declaration require an association to carry insurance covering the entire project, including the individual units. In townhome and single family developments, the advisability of having a master policy depends on the type of construction and the requirements of the legal documents. With townhouses, a master policy may be preferable to individual policies covering each dwelling. A master policy may cost less than all of the individual policies and also makes it easier to ensure adequate coverage and administer claims. Usually the developer purchases insurance that will be in effect at the time the owners elect the Board of Directors. Generally, the declaration specifies whether the insurance policy should be a master policy or whether it covers only common area improvements, thus encouraging owners to insure their own home. Co_ops operate like an apartment building and maintain a master policy for the entire building. Owners purchase what is typically a renter's policy to protect personal property.

Condominium unit owners should also obtain an owner's condominium policy covering the contents of the unit, personal liability and all additions and improvements. Such a policy covers loss or injury within the unit but does not include liabilities or damages occurring in the common area. The owner can obtain additional living expense endorsements and rental coverage. For a homeowners association, where individual policies are required instead of a master policy, association legal documents can require that minimum insurance limits and copies of certificates or policies be on file with the association.

Some master policies exclude rain damage to the interior of the unit unless the rain entered through a hole caused by wind_driven rain. Some master policies overlap or even contradict individual owner policies. This is where many conflicts arise between an owner and the Board. Therefore, individual owners must protect their personal property, furniture, fixtures, glass, additional living expenses, loss of rental income, personal liabilities and anything not covered by the master policy, otherwise they are self insured. Often the insurance coverage is broader than the association's documents require. This creates many disputes among associations, owners and their carriers.

The Board should be familiar with the extent of the coverage under its policy in order to budget for deductibles and association co_insured losses that must be paid out of pocket.

Types of Insurance

Liability Insurance. Liability insurance protects the Board and the members of the association from losses due to bodily injury or property damage caused by an occurrence covered by the insurance policy. Although liability insurance covers many areas, certain matters are generally excluded, i.e., automobiles, injury to employees, libel or slander, and contractual liability. Many exceptions can be covered under separate policies or additional riders. It is also a good idea to purchase an excess liability umbrella or insurance policy which can obtain millions of dollars of additional protection for a minimum premium. Several cases have held that where a personal injury judgment was entered against an association in excess of the policy limits, the individual owners had to make up the difference.

Flood Insurance. In designated flood hazard areas, flood insurance may be required by local lenders. Certain mortgage lenders offering government_backed loans required property located in flood plains to obtain flood insurance. More often than not, local ordinances require developers to create compensatory flood control and drainage systems that remove the property from the flood plain category. The flood plain maps should then be amended when the development is approved. Sometimes an association will be required to pursue a map amendment because the lenders require flood insurance and the developer did not have the map revised.

Workers' Compensation. Generally, carrying workers' compensation insurance is recommended whether or not the association has actual employees. Independent contractors are not employees and do not need coverage. However, sometimes because of a lapse in coverage, a canceled policy or a number of other possibilities, an injured worker, even though not technically an association employee, is considered one nevertheless. The amount of the premium is generally determined by the total employee payroll and is usually nominal. For the possible exposure, the investment in premiums is worth the protection.

Directors and Officers Insurance. Officers and directors of an association may be subject to personal liability for suits brought by owners and third parties. The association must obtain adequate insurance protection to cover its directors, officers and employees in order to get people to serve. This insurance generally does not cover liability for intentional acts or civil rights violations. Directors and officers policies have become increasingly expensive but are an absolute necessity.

Some policies do not cover officers and directors for liability from claims arising from actions taken while they were on the Board when the claims are made after they are no longer on the Board. The association should make sure that it obtains the broadest coverage possible. Of course, association documents generally indemnify officers and directors against personal liability that is not covered under the association's policy, as does the Illinois General Not For Profit Corporation Act. The problem is that the largest portion of the coverage is for legal defense. Even when a director or officer is indemnified, the cost of defending a large claim could bankrupt an association.

Lastly, most property management companies include standard provisions in their contracts to indemnify the manager for any wrongful acts of the Board, including providing legal defense.

Association_Owned Property. If the association owns property such as equipment, furnishings, pool furniture, pool cleaning equipment, etc., it should be insured to full replacement value under the policy. Standard "all risk" insurance policies may exclude theft of personal property. Property owned by the residents and owners is not covered by the association.

Replacement Cost Endorsement. Unless there is a special endorsement, a standard policy will depreciate a building in the event of loss so that the depreciated value is the extent of the coverage. A special endorsement should be included which provides coverage for the replacement value rather than depreciated value.

Inflation Endorsement. Coverage should also be included which provides insurance that automatically increases by a specified percentage in the event of rapid inflation.

Policy Exclusions. It is important to be aware of the exclusions under all policies. Generally, damage from termites, dry rot, underground water and flooding, sewer backups, building settling, electrical shorts and broken glass is not included. Under directors and officers policies, civil rights violations and most intentional actions are excluded.

Deductibles. Most associations carry a $1,000 or more deductible for any loss. This means the association pays any association loss up to $1,000 before the coverage kicks in. This is always an area of controversy, where damages to the common elements are caused by an owner and the cost of repair is below the deductible. The association insures the common elements and must underwrite the cost of repair, regardless of cause. Only in some instances, depending on the wording of a declaration, can a Board go after a negligent owner to recover the cost of a deductible.

Coinsurance. Most insurance policies require that a building be insured up to its full value or at least a substantial percentage of its full value. That is because the higher the value insured, the higher the premium. The insurance company does not want to be in the position of having to pay more for a building than the amount of the insurance carried. Therefore, the insurance companies require that an association carry 80% or more of the value of the building in casualty insurance. If an association fails to carry that much insurance, the coinsurance clause says it will be penalized and become a coinsurer. Generally, the association should carry insurance in the amount of 100% of the replacement value of the improvements.

Conclusion

The Board has a duty to keep the members informed as to what is and what is not covered by the insurance policies carried by the association. Owners who rent their units should carry rental loss insurance, as well as additional liability coverage. All unit occupants, whether owners or renters, should carry contents coverage under an owners or renters policy.

The biggest area of controversy arises when several different insurance companies are involved and a loss affects the common elements and the units. The dispute often concerns between what is association responsibility vs. what is owner responsibility. These arguments often must be settled by looking at the legal documents or by reviewing the statutory definitions. What further complicates matters is not a lack of coverage but an overlap or double coverage. Each of these disputes must be worked out on a case_by_case basis because not all insurance policies and declarations read the same.

Also, where a master policy fully insures the buildings and individual unit owners have their own policies, there may be over_insurance. This may lead to total recoveries exceeding the actual loss. It may also result in proration or division of the liability of the different carriers. This should be worked out among the carriers.

Section 12 of the Illinois Condominium Property Act sets out the requirements for insurance, and each carrier that writes insurance must draft its policies in conformance with these statutory provisions. For all other associations, the declaration or by_laws will generally state the insurance requirements.

While attempting to vigorously enforce association policies and protecting individual rights, a Board can run into claims of arbitrariness or lack of fairness. At all times, Board members must make a good faith effort to enforce the rules in compliance with the law, which is why any Board actions which are the least bit questionable should be scrutinized for their legality.

CHAPTER 15

▼

BOARD MEMBERS OR BORED MEMBERS: HOW TO RECRUIT AND RETAIN GOOD PEOPLE forCONDOMINIUM AND HOMEOWNER ASSOCIATION BOARDS

It is estimated that by the end of the century over 50% of all residential property will belong to some form of community association. Generally created as not_for_profit corporations, member-elected Boards of Directors are charged with administering the day_to_day affairs of these associations.

In light of the burden and responsibility of fiduciary duty imposed by case law and by statute, it is critical for associations to seek out and retain qualified individuals to oversee their property's fortunes, to keep it maintained in a first_class fashion and to prudently manage association funds.

However, it is highly unusual for a Board to go from one annual election to the next without being compelled to fill a vacancy. What is also becoming a problem is the mere slating of a sufficient number of qualified individuals to fill all the vacancies. This condition is increasing in epidemic proportions and can result in the deterioration and depreciation of the property. However, by observing the warning signs, by tightening up policies and procedures and by implementing innovative and efficient programs, this problem, if not entirely avoidable, can at least be minimized.

The Initial Board

The first Board of Directors can consist of former ad_hoc or transition committee members, reluctant recruits, ego_intensive opportunists and developer_tied appointees. How an association operates in its first year determines how and with whom the first generation of directors will be succeeded. Boards of Directors too often consist of do_gooders, people on a "power trip" or those who think they are the only ones intelligent enough to protect their investment.

Recruitment

The first objective in creating an effective Board of Directors is to seek out and recruit people with the right temperament, experience and philosophy. Look for these traits:

- People who have the ability to use prudent, sound business judgment;
- People who care about property values, resale and appreciation;
- People who are not afraid to make a decision; and
- People who are not narrowly focused on a "single" issue.

Once you find these individuals, appeal to their rational business sense. However, if all else fails, try flattery—or fear might be a great motivator. (If you don't serve, do you know what will happen?) Above all else, avoid narrow_minded people or those with only self_serving or selfish motives.

Defining Roles

Associations have two principal functions—acting as a government and as a business. The Board of Directors is charged with initiating legislation to govern day_to_day living, create restrictions on behavior, interpret and apply recorded covenants and punish offenders. Because the Board also is responsible for administering large sums of money, it must have strict policies on collecting revenue, seek out alternative methods of generating income, prudently solicit and review contract proposals and carry out the primary responsibility of maintenance.

Board members must be decision makers. Some of the best people to recruit are those willing to seek out or create preventive_type policies and those who are open_minded and will listen to the advice of paid professionals. Such individuals will not only create a more efficient operation, but also make the job more fulfilling and limit liability in certain areas.

Evolution of a Board Member

Directors generally begin their first term in a state either of apprehension or wild_eyed enthusiasm.

It is important that a leader emerge who can keep Board members calm throughout their term. At each meeting, the presiding officer should follow an agenda and limit questions from the audience so that the Board can efficiently conduct its business. The reluctant director will then sense that matters are under control and go along with the game plan.

The uncontrolled optimist, however, must be given small jobs and responsibilities to keep him or her busy with praise and pats on the head for a job well done. It is important to channel this energy in a positive direction in order to keep these types of people interested.

As a Board evolves as a unit, the leadership must find creative ways to keep people interested and avoid falling into a rut. Periodically changing the location of the meeting, offering refreshments, and having an annual dinner meeting or social event will keep the "team" concept alive.

Education

Board members will be more comfortable in their roles if they feel confident that they know what they are talking about when questions are asked. Numerous publications are available to educate and update directors on procedures and innovations in association administration. Associations should also invest in sending directors to professionally run seminars, conventions and classes in order to bring the dry, book_learned knowledge to life in a group setting.

Avoiding Burnout

The quickest way to alienate existing directors and discourage good people from running for the Board is to ignore the warning signs and just let an association drift. Consider these suggestions to keep people interested and involved:

1. Hold efficient, short meetings—Write a tight agenda and stick to it. Limit owner questions to a set time and do not allow maintenance requests to become part of an agenda. Keep control of the meeting and limit discussion to the matters before the Board. Inject a little humor and keep things moving. The goal should be a one_hour meeting.

2. Identify complacency and boredom—Frequently missed meetings, arbitrary behavior or bringing work to a meeting are telltale signs of a director at risk. Sometimes just talking to that person and offering a kind word can generate renewed interest.

3. Avoid turnoffs—Receiving calls at home, confrontations at the pool, long meetings, poor advice or inadequate performance by contractors or professionals and verbal challenges from owners who believe they were not informed of important decisions may cause Board members to re_think their priorities. Only a small minority are tenacious enough to overcome ongoing adversity and stick it out.

Conclusion

The key to getting and keeping Board members sometimes requires the Board to go back to basics:

1. Immediately after each election, have an information session to set goals and objectives for the coming year.

2. Meet with all professional advisors and contractors to review problem areas and improve service.

3. Hold a social event for the community during the year.

4. Seek out an editor and publisher for a newsletter.

5. Always keep in mind the demographics of the community; seniors, young marrieds, singles, etc., are interested in different activities.

6. Politely advise owners not to call you at home at an inappropriate time, but to call the manager.

7. Recruit a cross_section of the members to serve on the Board.

8.   Promote active committees in order to delegate the workload.

9.   Take the necessary steps to allay fears of personal liability, i.e., conduct reserve studies, adequately fund reserves, maintain appropriate insurance coverage, keep good minutes of meetings, practice preventive law and financial planning, keep the property looking good and make sure rules are reasonable and enforceable.

These are some of the ways to keep your association operating efficiently and happily. Remember, a property is only as good as its Board members.

CHAPTER 16

▼

USING COMMITTEES: OR HOW NOT TO DO IT ALL YOURSELF

The Illinois General Not For Profit Corporation Act and most governing documents for associations and by_laws for co_ops provide for the use of committees in order to assist the Board of Directors in the administration and operation of the property.

By not utilizing committees in delegating the workload, a Board is probably looking at a very high "burnout" rate for its directors.

Committees serve a number of purposes in the operation of an association:

1. They are an effective way to involve a multitude of people in the association.

2. They are good training grounds to groom future Board members.

3.   They are a means of utilizing the special talents
     of Board members and other members of the
     community, i.e., finance committee, mainte-
     nance committee, etc.

4.   They are an efficient means of getting a commit-
     ment from interested and active members who
     do not desire or have the necessary time to com-
     mit to Board obligations.

5.   They are the best way to delegate and spread
     some of the workload so that a Board is not
     overwhelmed.

The Board can appoint a committee chairperson, who
can then select the members of the committee from a pool
of interested members.Section 108.40 of the Illinois
General Not For Profit Corporation Act designates two
different types of committees.

First is the "full authority" committee that must (a) consist of a majority of directors, (b) be selected by the majority of the Board and (c) have at least two directors on the
committee, as it is defined. This type of committee has the
power to bind the association to policies, contracts, etc.
However, this format is rarely used because the Board as a
whole usually wishes to be in control of making association
policy and sometimes directors and officers insurance does
not cover committee members who are not directors.

Second is the "limited authority" committee or com-
mission which has no authority to bind the association
and is merely a recommending body. This is the most
common type of committee; it functions under the
direction of the Board and does not require directors as
members of the committee. Because of liability and control issues, this is the best way for a Board to structure

committees. Although in a strict statutory sense "limited authority" committees are designated "commissions," they are most often called committees and shall be, for the purpose of this article.

Whether "full authority" or "commissions," these bodies are divided into three classes:

1. Standing committees
2. Special committees
3. Subcommittees

A standing committee operates from year to year and is assigned specific tasks at the direction of the Board. It generally has a full agenda of ongoing activities that extends from year to year. Typically, standing committees include:

1. Finance—which prepares the budgets and advises the Board on special assessments and capital expenditures.

2. Maintenance—which reviews contract specifications, screens contractor bids, acts as a liaison between the contractor(s) and the Board, etc.

3. Buildings and Grounds—which walks the property periodically, prepares punchlists of maintenance items and works with the landscaper and snow removal contractors.

4. Judiciary—which hears the rule infraction complaints and conducts informal hearings.

5. Social—which plans social events when appropriate.

6. Newsletter—which prepares periodic communications for the community.

Special committees are appointed for limited and specific purposes and serve until they complete their designated tasks. Usually a Board will appoint a Rules Committee to prepare recommended rules and regulations, a Nominating Committee to screen and select candidates for the Board and supervise elections, a Pool Committee to supervise lifeguards and pool maintenance operations, an Insurance Committee to review insurance requirements and specifications, and various search committees to screen and hire professionals.

Lastly, subcommittees can be set up under the auspices of the other committees to handle small projects either on a singular or continuing basis. For example, the Buildings and Grounds Committee may seek to appoint a subcommittee to select paint colors or flower species, etc.

Obviously, the more people involved in the committee process, the more the work is spread out, which should result in efficient Board operations. It is critical under this scenario that limits of authority are clearly defined and a chain of command is established so an association is not victimized by a number of "loose cannons on a rolling deck."

All committees should ultimately be accountable to the Board of Directors by being included on meeting agendas and reporting on their activities. A Board should give clear direction as to each committee's scope of responsibility.

Each year after the new Board is elected, committees must be reappointed. Ideally, a committee should have a chairperson and vice_chairperson. Each chairperson should serve for two years and then be succeeded by the vice_chairperson. This allows for orderly transition, continuity of leadership, knowledge and experience, and avoids "burnout" and the creation of "kingdoms."

Committee meetings do not have to be opened to the membership, since they cannot bind the association to any of their decisions.

When a committee is not operating properly, either it is not being properly supervised by the Board or it has become a maverick. In either instance, the chairperson should be required to attend meetings and either account for deficient performance or be replaced. Allowing the situation to go on too long will ultimately result in either a non_functioning committee or resentment among the members. If a committee member, including the chairman, is not a team player, he or she should be replaced.

By following set guidelines and using good organizational skills, a Board can recruit and maintain Board members and not "bored" members.

CHAPTER 17

▼

THE ROLE OF THE ASSOCIATION ATTORNEY: REPRESENTING THE BOARD

An association attorney must be well-versed in numerous areas of law; be able to mediate differences between the Board and management, defend the association in a lawsuit, handle routine litigation and arbitrate covenant violations; be up-to-date on the Association's financial status; be available to review documents and attend special meetings; and be prepared to routinely counsel the Board on matters of policy and procedure.

Representing the Board of Directors of a condominium association is often compared to representing a municipal body, a corporation, a small business or a plethora of other entities. However, the Board remains a unique animal, requiring an attorney to have a good working knowledge of numerous areas of law.

First, the attorney must be familiar with applicable statutes: bankruptcy law, mortgage foreclosure law, land-lord/tenant law, the association's operating documents, etc. In addition, he or she must be familiar with the association's history, Board politics and the property's physical layout.

The attorney must also be a diplomat to balance the personal concerns and "causes" of individual Board members with the position of the managing agent and possibly with other accounts.

Finally, for most substantially sized associations, the attorney's office often acts as an agency for collecting delinquent assessments, monitoring accounts, negotiating payment plans, litigating evictions and advising the Board of its status.

By working closely with the association in its initial stages and with the new Board when it is elected, the attorney can help establish efficient operating procedures. In doing so, he or she will also help foster a long-term relationship with the client.

Discussed below are some areas of Board representation that are controversial and some recommended procedures for smoothing out trouble spots.

Establishing a Relationship

Frequent communication is required to maintain an effective relationship with the Board. If the association is new, it is advisable for the attorney to attend a number of meetings on a regular basis to monitor procedures and hopefully prevent long-term problems, such as potential litigation. To keep costs down, associations should consider determining a nominal monthly retainer fee for unlimited telephone calls.

Communication is also essential for generating other projects, such as developing opinion letters that interpret the declaration, resolutions, contracts, etc.

Fee Arrangement

An hourly rate should be established for corporate work and collections, and all work should be billed on a project-to-project basis. Collecting assessments on a contingency basis is improper, since attorney fees for collection of assessments are mandated by statute and by most declarations.

However, the attorney must gear his or her collection fee schedule to what can be obtained from most judges presiding over collection cases. Excessive billing on collection cases, especially when all sums may not actually be collected, will result in unnecessary out-of-pocket expenses for the association.

Board Procedures

The Board must comply with statutorily prescribed procedures governing notice prior to its open meetings (condominiums and all not-for-profit corporations) as well as the conduct of those meetings. The Board must also be aware of the circumstances under which it conducts a closed or "executive" session and that *all* voting must still take place at an open meeting. While exceptions to open meetings do exist, such as discussions concerning litigation, personnel matters and covenant violations, the failure to comply with notice and voting requirements makes the Board a ripe target for litigation on the basis of acting outside the scope of its authority.

The attorney often acts as an arbitrator for covenant violations. Disputes between neighbors that boil over into association-wide problems can sometimes be handled objectively by the attorney by bringing the affected parties to a meeting, reviewing their versions of the facts and making a recommendation. However, one caveat about nuisance complaints is that the Board is not the police department. "Classic" neighbor disputes should be referred to the appropriate authorities, and not handled by the Board.

Attorneys must always keep in mind that Board members are deemed to be fiduciaries and need to be advised accordingly. The Board must have errors and omissions coverage, notwithstanding the limitation-of-liability provisions in most declarations. Further, in condominium associations containing more than 30 units, a fiduciary bond is required of all directors, officers and agents handling association funds [§18(b)(13)(h)].

If the Board is named as a defendant in a lawsuit, the attorney should first determine whether there is insurance coverage for the defense. If not, as with contractual disputes or mortgage foreclosures, the attorney should file the appropriate documents and undertake a defense.

In summary, the attorney should be consulted regarding adopting written resolutions for establishing policies, reviewing rules and regulations, monitoring hearing procedures for levying fines and handling homeowner complaints.

Counseling the Board

The primary role of the association attorney is keeping the Board out of trouble. By encouraging open lines of communication, his goal is twofold. First, he can encourage the Board to adopt a preventive-law philosophy whereby little problems are referred immediately before they expand into large, expensive ones. Second, he must always make sure the Board is acting within the scope of its authority and in compliance with the statutes, declaration and by-laws. The most horrifying experience for Board members is to be sued individually for ultra vires actions, which are outside the scope of errors and omissions insurance coverage. The association is also barred from underwriting the defense costs of individuals in such cases.

If the attorney encourages the Board to consult with counsel to render a written opinion or to interpret the law and/or the documents when problems arise, the Board will learn to protect itself by acting diligently. The underlying objective is to teach the Board to use "sound business judgment" in all of its dealings.

Attorney as Parliamentarian

Most associations require their attorneys to attend annual and special meetings of the homeowners to assure that the meetings are conducted properly. Such meetings include annual elections, budget reviews, referenda, etc. The meetings themselves should be conducted along the guidelines of a simplified version of Robert's Rules of Order, and should include a written agenda.

One must remember that although Board meetings are open to association members and the owners are permitted to record the proceedings, there is no requirement that attendees be allowed to participate. Members must be constantly reminded that it is a "Board" meeting and the Board members are their elected representatives. However, as a matter of good public relations, some limited amount of time should be set aside prior to or just after the regular business portion of the meeting for homeowner input. The attorney will often be consulted on issues of appropriate proceedings and proper conduct of attendees.

Reviewing Documents

When the association is involved in litigation or some other potentially costly proceeding, the initial year of operation is usually its most expensive in terms of legal fees, which arise primarily from document preparation and review and the establishment of policy guidelines and procedures.

Using the preventive-law approach, the association attorney should make sure his or her client has a well-drafted set of standard agreements for the contractors who handle the association's snow removal, landscaping, management, etc. However, once the form-agreement has been prepared and implemented, it need only be reviewed periodically to update specifications.

Although competitive bidding for services is not required, "sound business doctrine" dictates that services be priced and compared prior to offering a contract and that the contract's format meet the attorney's approval.

Corporate Compliance

The association attorney should be named as the registered agent to the corporation so that in the event of litigation, such as a mortgage foreclosure or personal injury, the attorney will receive the earliest notification. Secondly, if the association is an Illinois not-for-profit corporation, the attorney will file annual reports to keep the corporation in good standing.

Changes in the Law

As in every other area of practice, the association attorney must stay abreast of the frequent changes in statutes and case law. The attorney should advise the Board of any changes and recommend whether the governing documents need to be amended or if the Board should revise any of its policies and procedures.

The attorney should consult specialized publications, such as law reporters, as well as the revision of any state statutes and local ordinances, to stay abreast of current legislative and judicial trends.

In preparing and filing amended documents, the attorney must always be sure that the express requirements of the law and the declaration are complied with, such as having the appropriate majority approve the amendments, giving notice to first mortgagees, etc.

Reviewing Insurance Coverage

One of the largest areas of controversy faced by the Board is whether a repair is the responsibility of the association or of an individual owner. This will more often than not arise in the context of insurance coverage for a casualty loss.

The strict requirements of the law and the declaration regarding responsibility for repairs will often be circumvented by the broader coverage of the master insurance policy. This is further complicated when the association has a large deductible. What often occurs when there is a loss is that the owner's insurance carrier will deny coverage, even though it has responsibility. The association's master policy will defer, but because it is not an express requirement of the declaration, damages will be for an amount less than the deductible. The Board and the association attorney must be prepared to untangle this mess and determine whether to charge the association or the owner for repairs, or be prepared to work out a compromise.

Prudent representation by the attorney also includes an annual review all of insurance and advising the Board about deductibles, extended coverage, flood insurance, worker's compensation, etc. The Board should be fully advised to the extent and scope of potential areas of exposure.

Working with Management

Most associations are managed either by an independent company or by a Board employee, although sometimes the Board itself manages the property. Regardless, the attorney must have an effective working relationship with management. This facilitates timely and important communication and generates results when corporate and collection work are needed.

Obviously, the attorney assuming the role of the diplomat is crucial in such situations, particularly if a problem arises due to a managerial error. Although the Board is the attorney's client, management actually has the most significant influence on the association's day-to-day operations. The attorney always needs to balance the Board's concerns with those of management (particularly when they are the same!).

Conclusion

These are but a fraction of the types of problems an association attorney must confront on a daily basis. Needless to say, representing a condominium association is a challenging test of a lawyer's versatility. However, it is a rewarding area of law and one that has grown into a widely recognized specialty. What has not been discussed here are the ever-burgeoning areas of litigation involving associations and covenant enforcement, delinquent collection, procedures, warranty defects, etc.

By the end of the decade, approximately 50% of the nation's people will live in housing governed by common-interest community associations. Those associations will create a significant demand on the legal community to provide quality legal services, competent representation and counsel, and expert solutions to complex problems.

CHAPTER 18

▼

DEALING WITH A CRISIS: THE LAWYER'S ROLE

When disaster strikes a co-operative or an association, the Board must react quickly to implement damage control. A crisis management plan should already be in place, not created at the time it is actually needed.

While practical problems need to be addressed on an ongoing basis, sometimes the legal consequences of a disaster have far-reaching results. Therefore, crises of all sizes need a "legal preparedness strategy" in place.

One of the roles of the Board's attorney is to discuss crises communications and planning issues with the Board and management. Even trained professional managers or experienced Board members are not necessarily schooled in all of the legal ramifications and financial risks associated with legal proceedings.

Preventive Law and Situation Planning

The attorney has the responsibility to communicate with the Board what legal services are available in terms of legal consultation and advice. When so informed, the Board is prepared to seek legal advice in a timely manner when a controversy arises. This allows the attorney to be brought in at the earliest possible stage to help limit the scope of the problem before it gets out of hand.

The attorney should be consulted for help before a situation becomes a crisis; when it is still a minor controversy, plans can be initiated for the prevention of more serious problems.

For example, updating rules and regulations, legal review and frequent communication with all owners and residents eliminates many problem areas before they arise.

Components of Crisis Preparedness

To prepare a plan to effectively respond to emergencies, a Board must address:

- Identifying a problem that is in fact a crisis (who, what, where).
- How to effectuate an active visible response (how).
- Handing the situation expeditiously (when).
- Preparing to deal with the interruption of essential services.
- Showing compassion and providing assistance to the parties involved.
- Presenting consistent and unambiguous communication.
- Following up on the initial response(s).
- Keeping the owners informed.
- Issuing written communication to the members and/or a press release, if appropriate.

The Role of the Attorney

The Board should be aware of what role each member—the directors, the manager, the accountant, etc.—plays. By establishing the scope of authority in which the lawyer can initiate action without going back to the Board for further direction, the Board eliminates duplication of effort and overlap.

The attorney should be responsible for:

- Analyzing the situation and making sure it is in fact a crisis and not an over-reaction to a problem.
- Having a pre-planning session with the Board/Manager, outlining various situations and the appropriate response(s).
- Identifying who is the proper spokesperson for the Board and the extent of his or her authority.
- Establishing guidelines and specifics for appropriate communication.
- Diffusing the emotions as soon as possible.
- Preparing appropriately drafted communications to be distributed to owners and any third parties (media, municipality, police, etc.).
- Recommending agencies, contractors, officials, etc. that can offer assistance.
- Meeting as needed to direct strategy and refine tactics.
- Sending concluding recommendations with advice to deal with additional consequences or preventive techniques to avoid a repeat of the situation.

What is most important is that the attorney be part of the "crisis management team" as much for the strategic planning as for legal solutions. Dealing with a crisis generally requires an instant analysis as to whether a bona fide state of emergency exists or whether a problem can merely be addressed in the ordinary course of business. A "drop everything" mentality cannot be applied to every situation, because if everything is a crisis, then nothing is a crisis!

The astute counselor must quickly learn to react to the different personalities of managers and Board members in order to tailor appropriate responses.

Lastly, the most important thing an attorney can do is to be frank—not just telling the client what he or she wants to hear, but offer good, sound, objective advice. By pre-planning and utilizing a systematic approach to problem-solving, the crisis itself can be contained, consequential damages can be minimized and legal expenses can be kept under control.

CHAPTER 19

▼

KEEPING YOUR LEGAL EXPENSES
UNDER CONTROL

As Associations age and are confronted with massive
maintenance expenses and increasing assessment levels, one
of the first places targeted for cutbacks is the legal budget.
Unfortunately, legal expenses are not a luxury that can
always be reduced or eliminated. What a diligent Board
should do, however, is to implement certain practices to
work with legal counsel to reduce risks and liabilities. By
maintaining contact with your lawyer and having him or
her involved in various aspects of decision making, you are
buying legal health insurance; that is you pay a small premium to avoid a catastrophic loss. Here are 10 ways to
keep that one intangible in the budget under control:

1.   **Help your lawyer by practicing "preventive
      law."** Ask questions or obtain a legal opinion for

controversial matters before they get ugly or turn into unnecessary litigation.

2. **Solicit written legal opinions.** Minimize the Board's risks and liabilities by compiling and categorizing written legal opinions in a looseleaf binder. This becomes a handy reference guide for current and future Boards and avoids duplication.

3. **Have your attorney review large contacts.** The biggest mistake a Board can make is to sign an outside contractor's standard agreement without having it reviewed by counsel. Performance standards, acts of default, termination, etc. are all "litigation landmines" if not properly drafted. Spending a few hundred dollars on a contract review and even a revision can save thousands of dollars in case of a dispute.

4. **Send rules and regulations to be reviewed.** Unenforceable, illegal or discriminatory rules are the best way to wind up in court. No one knows an Association better than the people who live there. Rules and regulations should be drafted and updated annually by the Board or a committee. However, the Association's attorney should review them for legal content before adoption.

5. **Turn over delinquencies promptly.** Although an Association should try and handle as many early steps in the collection process as possible (reminder letters, phone calls), once the account is over 60 days old, it should be referred to legal counsel. The older the receivable, the harder it is to collect and the greater the likelihood of a mortgage foreclosure wiping out the Association's lien.

6. **Provide complete information when a complex legal matter or litigation arises.** One of the greatest wastes of money is paying legal fees for researching and investigating facts already in the possession of the Board or the manager. Prior to commencing any complex situations, meet with the lawyer and obtain a list of necessary documents and information essential to the file. This can reduce delays and provide significant savings.

7. **Have your attorney serve as registered agent for the corporation.** Many Boards think they are saving money by having the president or the manager serve as the registered agent. Little do they realize that the delays in receiving notices, the duplication of effort and the legal exposure they are open to not only create unnecessary risks, but ultimately results in little, if any, cost savings.

8. **Obtain status reports and updates before Board meetings.** In so doing, the Board can review and vote on any matters related to a legal situation in an educated and efficient manner. The Board can have the attorney attend, if necessary, so there is an economy of effort and dollars by having all of the Board members' questions answered in a one-hour session.

9. **Get a quote for projects.** Most experienced attorneys can quote a range or flat fee for most projects, with the exception of complex litigation. Just as managers contact contractors to obtain prices and estimates, the association's attorney can provide input in preparing the budget.

10. **Last and most important, keep lines of communication open.** One big mistake made by Boards is not asking the simple question. People are afraid to call their legal counsel because of costs. Having and using a lawyer to "run Board business" and "administer its government," is a cost of doing business that is no different from using management, maintenance, accounting services, etc. Actually, an ongoing legal relationship can save thousands of dollars over time.

Although utilizing legal counsel is a necessity for any prudent Board, it does not have to be a "budget buster." Sensible communication and direction is the key to having your lawyer make sure that little problems stay that way.

CHAPTER 20

▼

ACCESS TO ASSOCIATION RECORDS

Since the early '70s, allowing public access to records and files has become a mandatory obligation of government (Freedom of Information Act), subject to certain limited exceptions. What are the rights of an owner in a condominium, co-operative or homeowner's association as to examining the books and records?

The Illinois General Not For Profit Corporation Act requires that "each corporation shall keep correct and complete books and records of account and shall also keep minutes of the proceedings...books and records of a corporation may be inspected by any member entitled to vote, or that member's agent or attorney, for any proper purpose at any reasonable time."

The Illinois Condominium Property Act also provides that the records of a condominium association be open to inspection by all members or their designated representatives. If the Board fails to provide records properly requested, the owner may seek the appropriate relief, including an award of attorneys' fees and costs. On the other hand, the Board does have the right to establish procedures and set limitations, including the recovery of all costs to be incurred.

Thus, a duty is imposed upon an association to provide almost unlimited accessibility to association records. This is, in effect, a two-fold obligation, as the Board of Directors is ultimately responsible for reasonable access to the books and records, as well as being vicariously liable for the manager or agent hired for the purpose of maintaining them.

However, in spite of the appearance of uncontrolled accessibility, the Board can still impose certain reasonable restrictions to maintain control of the situation. Initially, the law imposes a similar if not far greater duty upon public bodies for citizen access to public records. This right is guaranteed by federal and state statute, as well as the Constitution of the State of Illinois. Even public bodies are permitted to impose certain restrictions on accessibility.

For the purpose of establishing a uniform and open policy in order to comply with the intent of the applicable statutes, Boards should adopt the following policy:

The following requirements are hereby established for the inspection of the ABC Association's records:

1. A notice of intent to inspect must be submitted in writing to the Board of Directors or its duly authorized agent at least 24 hours prior to the planned inspection.

2. The notice must specify with particularity which records are to be inspected and whether reproduction and mailing of copies is sufficient.

3. The owner requesting the records must state with particularity the purpose for which the records are to be reviewed.[2]

4. All records shall be inspected at the registered office of the association between the hours of 9:00 a.m. and 5:00 p.m., Monday through Friday.

5. At the discretion of the Board of Directors, or its agent, certain records may only be inspected in the presence of a Board member or employee or agent.

6. The person(s) requesting access shall not disrupt the ordinary business activities of the registered office or its employees during the course of inspection.

7. No actual records may be removed from the office without the express written consent of the Board of Directors.

8. When applicable, all costs of inspection shall be borne by the person requesting access. In the event the person reviewing the records is desirous of making photocopies, all costs of copying will be incurred by the person requesting same.[3] The Board reserves the right to

---

2. In *Meyer v. Board of Managers of Harbour House, et al.*, 164 Ill. Dec. 460, 1991, the court held that delinquency reports and itemized bills for legal services could be reviewed subject to the owner showing a proper purpose.

3. In the case of *Winter v. Playa del Sol*, 353 So.2d 598, 1977, the court held that "the right to inspect records would in many cases be valueless without the right to make copies."

request a cash deposit for copy costs to be incurred if it is reasonable to anticipate that there will be a large number of copies.

9. There are some limitations on access. Consistent with an individual's right to privacy and applicable law, the following records will not be made available without the express written consent of the Board of Directors:

A. Minutes and/or notes from Executive Sessions.

B   Minutes of Administrative Hearings pertaining to the imposition of fines, late fees or other punitive disposition.

C. Records whose disclosure would violate a constitutional or statutory provision or applicable public policy.

D. Records whose disclosure could result in a discernable harm to the association or any of its members.

E. Personnel records.

F. Interoffice memoranda.

G. Litigation files.

H. Preliminary data, information or investigations which have not been formally approved by the Board of Directors, such as prospective contractor bids.

I. Records whose disclosure may result in an invasion of personal privacy, breach of confidence or privileged information.

J. Records whose disclosure would unreasonably interfere with or disrupt the operation of the association.

K.   Records whose access results in a private harm or damage that outweighs the right to access.

10.   The association is under no obligation for providing any additional information other than that which is required by law.

By adopting guidelines, the association can operate with as little disruption as possible. In addition, professional management companies hired by the Board will have the express authority to limit such reviews to properly submitted requests. Though the Board of Directors has a legal obligation to permit unimpaired access to statutorily mandated records, it can limit its exposure for arbitrary, capricious or reckless conduct. In turn, the owner will be provided with all of the necessary data to accomplish his or her purpose in making the request. It is only when an association does not have a consistent and even-handed policy that a bitter conflict or litigation may result.

CHAPTER 21

▼

TOOLS FOR A BETTER BOARD MEETING; WHY DO THESE PEOPLE ACT THIS WAY?

If you have occasion to attend a number of association Board meetings, you will undoubtedly realize that this is a great way to study human behavior. The range of intellectual levels, fashions, emotional outpourings and exposition of minutia would be a great topic for a Ph.D. dissertation. However, if you are a property manager or a Board member, you may sometimes wonder what is going on to make people behave the way they do.

In attempting to regulate or even change behavior, one must first understand what causes it. This author has always felt that to be effective, one cannot expect every person to behave in the same manner. People are different. You must "take each person as you find him or her." Walk around in their moccasins, if you will…!

The dynamics of the group present at a Board meeting will be influenced by the topic of discussion. Serious financial problems or building defects may create a great deal of stress before the meeting even begins. What is probably most disturbing for anyone in attendance is a rambling, out-of-control coffee klatch, where it takes four hours to hire a painter. Instead of diffusing tempers, this will only ignite them.

Following are some guidelines which should help in fulfilling the ideals and principles of "communal living" and make life better for all parties concerned.

1.   **Prepare an agenda and stick to it**. If people sense that a meeting is not going to be controlled, they will control it. By having an agenda and following it, the president can conduct the business portion of the meeting efficiently and expeditiously. By avoiding cross-discussion, matters not on the agenda or maintenance complaints, the Board meeting, under most scenarios, should last about an hour.

2.   **Set aside a time for homeowner questions and limit that time**. A Board meeting is not a place to ask to have a leak fixed. If the property is professionally managed, calls regarding such complaints should be taken during the day by the manager. If a homeowner is not getting action, only then should the issue be brought to the Board. If limited time is set aside for the members to ask questions or speak out (especially at the beginning), the meeting can then follow the prepared agenda without further interruption.

3.   **Sort out the bid proposals in executive or closed session before bringing them to the open meeting**. All contracts must be voted on at meetings open to the members. But, the members do not have to sit through the

sorting and debating portion. An item entitled "_____ contract" should be included under new business at a Board meeting so the finalist(s) can be discussed and approved in public.

4.   **Managers are paid to advise, so advise!** Unhappy homeowners and insecure Board members can smell blood. When the property manager is unsure and wishywashy, they will move in for the kill. Attention property managers! Do your homework and take a stand! If you are confident in your opinion because you have thoroughly reviewed a matter, it is your job to make a recommendation. That is what you are being paid to do. If the Board doesn't like your opinion, they can vote it down and you can send a CYA (Cover Your Assets) letter. However, if you are unprepared, unsure and are unable to take a position, be assured either the Board or the members will make your life miserable.

5.   **A president is a benevolent dictator.** "Too much democracy is a dangerous thing." The president must control the meeting, and control does not license to abuse. The president should be calm, professional and firm in administering a Board or homeowners meeting. Follow the agenda, ask people in attendance, politely, not to interrupt and do not let Board members ramble on incessantly or try to control the meeting. A common mistake for Board presidents is that they believe they have all sorts of power that actually lies with the Board itself. However, the power they really should exercise is the ability to control and run a professional meeting.

6.   **Board members or bored members?** Do not let your directors burn out from stress or lack of commitment. Even veteran Board members reach a point of saturation.

Assign tasks to people to suit their talents. Delegate as much as possible to committees, individual directors and volunteers. Most importantly, be sensitive and open to individual complaints so the Board can work as a team before a director resigns in disgust. Rambling, uncontrolled Board meetings that seemingly last forever are the fastest way to burn out directors.

If the association's goal is to run a business, it must adopt the principles of a business. If the Board members act as fiduciaries for the members of the association, then they should take their job seriously, but not too seriously. An occasional social hour in lieu of a meeting, rather than using the meeting as a social hour, can go a long way toward addressing questions before they become problems and motivate homeowners and Board members to work together. If Board meetings are reactive, hyper intensive shouting sessions or extended sewing circles, the association will be unable to reach its primary goal—to improve and maintain the quality of life for its members and enhance property values.

CHAPTER 22

▼

COLLECTION POLICY AND PROCEDURES FORCONDOMINIUMS AND HOMEOWNERS ASSOCIATIONS

The Board must have a strict collection policy in place in order to deal effectively with delinquent owners. The law has established certain procedures for the collection of delinquent assessments in order to provide Associations with quick and cost effective ways of recovering the unpaid assessments, costs and fees.

However, within any system, there are certain givens:

        A.   No two cases are alike.

        B.   For every rule there is an exception.

        C.   The faster you attack a problem, the quicker the result.

        D.   Frequent communication is essential.

E.   Payment plans and work outs for first time delinquents are strongly encourage.

F.   Never send partial payments back unless they prejudice your case.

The following is a step-by-step outline of the procedures for establishing an effective collection policy.

PHILOSOPHY

It is crucial that accounts be turned over for collection promptly, in order to stay one step ahead of a mortgage foreclosure. Once the mortgage lender files suit and completes the foreclosure, they obtain a Sheriff's Deed. If the association has not begun to proceed with an eviction or obtained possession of a unit, rented it out and collected rent to offset the delinquent account, it will needlessly have to write off a bad debt.

FIRST NOTICE OF COLLECTION

In accordance with the Federal Fair Debt Collection Act, the association must notify a delinquent that they have thirty (30) days from the date of the first notice to demand verification (a breakdown). They can also request a payment plan. Also, all correspondence and notices to delinquents must be sent out disclosing the delinquent's rights or the sender can be subject to the payment of penalties and a delinquent's legal fees.

At the early stage, a payment plan will generally have the account cleared up in a very short period of time. To refuse an offer of payment may reduce your effectiveness. If the association takes a hard-line the first time an account is delinquent, it will probably have difficulty throughout the processing of the file and may force the delinquent to default on their mortgage. A payment plan for a "first-time" delinquent will usually result in cooperation and end the problem. However, accepting a payment plan does not mean accepting less than 100 cents on the dollar.

TRACT BOOK SEARCH

In order to commence collection proceedings, a tract book search (mini title search) should be ordered to verify ownership, mortgage lender(s), suits pending, other lien-holders, etc. The cost is charged back to the delinquent.

30-DAY NOTICE

Once the tract book search is received, proceed with sending an Illinois statutory 30-day notice to terminate possession, which begins the eviction process.

LIEN

A lien should also be recorded against the property in order to cloud the title in the event of a sale or refinance of a mortgage and to protect the Association's interest in case of a bankruptcy and/or foreclosure.

EVICTION

An action in forcible entry and detainer (eviction) is filed after the 30-day notice has run and payment is not received. A complaint is filed in the circuit court where the property is located and a summons is placed with the Sheriff's Office to be served on the delinquent(s).

The defendants must be brought within the jurisdiction of the court by being served with a copy of the complaint and summons. A court date is selected about 30 days after the first filing date.

If the owners have disappeared or are avoiding service, then the case must be continued an additional 21 days in order to do a Notice By Posting or the service of a second or "alias" summons. If the case proceeds on a notice by posting, you can only obtain possession of the unit, but not a personal money judgment against the delinquent.

Once the final court date arrives, most cases proceed as a "default" because the debtor generally does not show up. The court will enter an order terminating the owner's right of possession of the unit and award it to the association. If the defendant does appear, a trial will e held and the association must present evidence and witnesses in order to prove their case.

If the owner is still occupying the unit, the court will issue a "stay" for a minimum of 60 days before the Sheriff can be directed to evict them. There are some judges who insist on longer "stay" dates up to 120 days.

If a unit is leased out, the Board can demand that all future rents be paid to the association by the renter, or it can have the Sheriff evict the renter.

Once the unit is vacant, the association secures possession by changing the locks, renting the unit out and collecting rent to be applied against the delinquency.If you are renting out a unit, you may enter into a written lease for up to 13 months. However, units should not be leased out if the mortgage lender has commenced foreclosure proceedings and has already purchased the unit at a Sheriff's sale.

The entire eviction process can take a minimum of three months if all the factors are in place and the unit has been abandoned, or six to seven months if the unit is still occupied by the owner and they refuse to cooperate. However, it must be pushed along quickly in order to avoid losing out to a foreclosing mortgage holder.

MORTGAGE FORECLOSURE

The lien of the first mortgagee is superior to an association's assessment lien, which means that if they foreclose and there are no other bidders at the sale, the lender will purchase the unit for the amount of their lien and the association's lien is wiped out. Usually, the only chance of recovering the assessments is by renting out the unit after an eviction or determining that the foreclosure was defective.

Once the foreclosure is completed, the lender is only obligated to begin paying assessments from the first day of the month following the Sheriff's sale. They do not have to pay any past due assessments from before that date.

If all goes well, an association can collect enough rent, while monitoring the foreclosure, in order to pay off the delinquency, all costs and fees.

If the lender gets title before an association can collect all the back assessments, any deficiency can be lost unless the owner is located and is subject to a monetary judgment. Unfortunately, many people who lose their homes in foreclosure disappear. Secondly, they often file a Bankruptcy…

BANKRUPTCY

The association's assessment lien on the property is a non-dischargeable obligation, which means the association can still get paid.If the debtor files a Chapter 7, he should be persuaded to re-affirm his debt or else the association should petition the Bankruptcy Court to award the association the right to seek possession of the unit.

If the debtor files a Chapter 13 or debt reorganization, he must continue to pay current assessments, but the outstanding balance can be paid over a period of time. Most plans run 36-60 months. Often the debtor does not pay current assessments, so a petition must be filed with the court to allow an eviction to collect post-petition assessments. The association can insist upon being named as a priority creditor in order that it be paid off in a more expeditious manner. However, a large number of Chapter 13's fail, and once you receive notice of dismissal, you can proceed.

Lastly, if the debtor does file Bankruptcy (Chapter 7) after a foreclosure, the association must write off the balance.

CONCLUSION

In conclusion, there are many intangible factors that one cannot count on, such as debtors hiring attorneys to defend the case, counterclaims, extenuating circumstances at the time of purchase, bookkeeping errors, lost payments, etc.

You can help yourself by prompt turnover of delinquents to legal counsel, being reasonable at the initial stage, and most of all, understanding the process.

CHAPTER 23

▼

FIRST RIGHT OF REFUSAL
FOR CONDOMINIUMS:
PROTECTION OR ILLUSION

In 1960, the Illinois Supreme Court held that a cooperative housing community could enforce a restrictive covenant which provided that if a member sought to sell his or her unit, the association should, upon receipt of proper notice, have 12 months in which to purchase that member's interest, at the price either fixed in the notice or by agreement. If the right was not exercised within that period, then the membership could be sold on the open market. *Gale v. York Center Community Cooperative*, 21 Ill.2d 86, 171 N.E.2d 30, 1960.

Although this case established the precedent of the preemptive right, or right of first refusal, in Illinois, the concept was promoted primarily for cooperative housing developments which were fairly common at that time. The right of first refusal has since been extended to condominium associations.

A cooperative, or "co-op," is a corporation or trust established for the purpose of communally owning and maintaining property. The interests of the members are represented by shares of stock or ownership and entitle the members to the perpetual occupancy of their apartments and common areas. Membership is generally valued in terms of the payoff balance of a mortgage on the entire premises divided by the number of apartments, plus a factoring in of additional consideration for the common areas and the overall market value. If an owner walked away from his or her apartment, the remaining members would still be responsible for the entire outstanding loan balance, with or without that defaulting owner's contribution. Thus, the purpose of the "preemptive right" was to allow the remaining group of owners the absolute right to screen and even reject a potential member, if there was even an unrealistic belief that the proposed member might be a detriment to the community or pose a financial risk for the remaining members.

The Illinois Supreme Court weighed the "utility of the restraint as compared with the injurious consequences that will flow from its enforcement. If accepted social and economic considerations dictate that a partial restraint is reasonably necessary for their fulfillment, such a restraint should be sustained." The ruling in *Gale v. York Center, et al.* became the rule in Declarations of Covenants established for a majority of condominium associations developed since the adoption of the Illinois Condominium Property Act in 1963.

However, the legality of this covenant running with the land as it applies to all forms of property ownership is clouded by the probability and practicality of enforcement. This is further complicated by the dictates of the mortgage market and may in all likelihood be headed for "legal extinction."

A typical first right of refusal reads as follows:

Sale, Leasing or Alienation

Sale or Lease. Any Unit Owner other than the Trustee who wishes to sell or lease his Unit Ownership (or any lessee of any Unit wishing to assign or sublease such Unit) shall give the Board not less than thirty (30) days prior written notice of his intent to sell or lease and subsequently, the terms of any contract to sell or lease, entered into subject to the Board's opinion as set forth hereinafter together with a copy of such contract, the name, address and financial and character references of the proposed purchaser or lessee and such other information concerning the proposed purchaser or lessee as the Board may reasonably require. The giving of such notice shall constitute a warranty and representation by the giver thereof that he believes such offer, and all information contained in said notice, to be bona fide, true and correct in all respects. The members of the Board acting on behalf of the other Unit Owners shall at all times have the first right and option to purchase or lease such Unit Ownership upon the same terms, which option shall be exercisable for a period of thirty (30) days following the date of receipt of such notice of contract. If said option is not exercised by the Board within said thirty (30) days, the Unit Owner (or lessee) may, at the expiration of said thirty (30) day period and at any time within ninety (90) days after the expiration of said period, proceed to consummate the sale (or sublease or assignment of) such Unit Ownership to the proposed purchaser or lessee named in such notice upon the terms specified therein. If the Unit Owner (or lessee) fails to close said proposed sale or lease transaction within said ninety (90) days, the Unit Ownership shall again become subject to the Board's right of first refusal as herein provided.

The problems of strict compliance with the aforestated provision are multi-faceted.

First, most owners do not contact the Board of a condominium association for an express waiver of the preemptive right, until long after the required tine period elapses and usually just prior to the closing date of the sale.

As a practical matter, should an association expend its time and resources, as well as the possibility of substantial legal fees, seeking injunctive relief in order to void a sale for the owner's mere indiscretion of not sending adequate advance notice? Further, is a court going to terminate a sale to a qualified purchaser of a condominium and reverse the positions of the parties, merely on the basis of an owner's neglect in not seeking prior consent? It is unlikely that a court would not "balance the equities" and refuse to grant the injunctive relief sought after considering the potential hardship.

Secondly, most declarations have the additional requirement that the Board of Directors of the association must obtain 2/3 or 3/4 of the owners' approval within a specific time frame in order to authorize the Board to exercise this right.

As a practical matter, this type of majority is at best difficult to obtain even on the most significant issues. To obtain the necessary majority of owners to authorize the Board to utilize substantial sums from the operating budget or levy a special assessment to fund the purchase under the option requires an enormous amount of legwork.

Third, aside from the practical difficulties of enforcement, recent case law has eroded the former "iron-clad" position of these types of covenants, particularly as it pertains to blanket exclusions without the association having to show cause for exercising it.

In *Phillips v. Hunters Trails Community Association*, 685 F2d 184, 1982, the Seventh Circuit held that the association's exercise of the right of first refusal was racially motivated and constituted both a violation of the Civil Rights Act of 1966 as well as the Fair Housing Act. An award of punitive damages by the trial court was affirmed. This opinion then opens the door for an action against a Board whenever it acts arbitrarily, capriciously or in that case, illegally.

In *Berkley Condo, Assoc., Inc, v. Berkley Condo. Residences, Inc.*, 448 A2d 510, 1982, the New Jersey Supreme Court held that the New Jersey statute created a rebuttable presumption of unconscionability regarding provisions in association by-laws giving the association a right of first refusal to buy a condominium upon resale and was constitutional.

In both decisions, the reviewing courts found that it was clearly in the public interest to maintain unrestricted freedom in the transfer of real estate.

The reviewing court in the *Berkley* case concluded that "private property rights are not absolute and are always subject to the reasonable exercise of the police power."

Following these decisions, the 3rd District of Florida, which is a primary source of condominium-related litigation, struck down a right of first refusal clause as a restraint on alienation in *Aquarian Foundation, Inc, v. Shalom Houses, Inc.*, 448 So.2d 1166, 1984.

In this case, a unit owner sold her unit without association consent as required by the declaration, and the association actually sought to set aside the conveyance. The court found that since the Board could arbitrarily, capriciously and unreasonably withhold its consent, without a corresponding obligation to purchase or provide a purchaser, this constituted an invalid and unenforceable restraint.

Although this case can be viewed narrowly on its merits, a general trend may be developing overall. For years, cases such as the *Gale v. York Center* remained unassailable, even under the most questionable of circumstances. The prevailing philosophy extended far beyond the economics of the co-op and included social considerations. However, the practicality of unenforceability, coupled with recent successful court challenges, raises the entire issue of what was the intended purpose as it pertained to protection of the condominium association in general.

Illinois has also addressed this issue in the case of *Wolinsky v. Kadison*, 114 Ill. App.3d 527, 449 N.E.2d 151,

1984, when the court held, "Plainly, by exercising a right of first refusal, a condominium association prevents a prospective purchaser from buying a unit. We therefore believe that if a right of first refusal is exercised so that a prospective purchaser is unable to purchase a unit because of his or her race, religion, sex, sexual preference, marital status or national origin, the ordinance has been violated." (The ordinance in question is the anti-discrimination provision of the City of Chicago Condominium Ordinance.) Clearly, associations are now being held accountable for their actions, and exercise of the preemptive right can no longer be arbitrarily mandated by a Board of Directors without a showing of good cause.

In 1988, the Congress of the United States ratified the Fair Housing Amendments Act of 1989, which was adopted to promote and expand available housing. Discrimination based upon age, disability or family status was outlawed. A board considering whether to exercise its right of first refusal must now also look at other factors, such as protected classes, before it decides to buy or lease a unit.

It appears that there is a more prevailing concern by most resident owners with the problems in dealing with renters rather than enforcing preemptive rights on sales. In Illinois, §9.2 of the Illinois Condominium Property Act and Article IX of the Code of Civil Procedure permit the condominium association to utilize the remedy of forcible entry and detainer for violations of the covenants and §18 *et seq.* further binds renters as well as owners to the covenants and restrictions of records as well as the Act itself.

An association now clearly has adequate remedies available to control these situations, even within the shadow created by *Coventry Square Condo. Assn. v. Halpern*, 181

NJ. Superior Court 93, 1981, where the reviewing court struck down unreasonable and unnecessary restriction on renters or owners which created a limited class and violated the Equal Protection clause.

The amendments to the Illinois statute in conjunction with the governing document should be further expanded upon in the form of reasonable rules and regulations. This can foreclose any concerns about renters, real or imagined.

The final problem in enforcing the right of first refusal is created by the current market conditions dictated by the mortgage banking industry. Fannie May, FHA, VA, the secondary mortgage market, etc., are the order of the day. Conventional financing as it has evolved often prohibits the financing of a purchase of a unit situated in an association where the declaration gives the association the right of first refusal.

Creative draftsmanship, amendments to declarations and elaborate waiver letters have circumvented this problem to a certain degree. At best, associations are blindly waiving their rights in order to facilitate easy marketability on behalf of their membership and not interfere with the ability of an owner to sell his or her unit. Most developers are now omitting the right of first refusal from their initial documents in order to arrange for attractive block financing for new purchasers.

In conclusion, although an association may have a very elaborate provision for right of first refusal in its Declaration, it cannot practically enforce it. An anxious seller of a unit does not want it enforced and a trial court is unlikely to overturn an arms-length transaction if the association is not consulted in advance, unless the association can show irreparable harm. Many Board members operate under the illusion that the preemptive right offers some type of protection. However, in the long run, it is often practically unenforceable and in all likelihood should be automatically waived in most instances. The Board that is seriously concerned about the regulation of conduct and oblivious of its residents would be better off directing its time and energy to a well drafted, enforceable set of rules and regulations.

CHAPTER 24

▼

LEASING UNITS

Every owner should consider a number of important items when leasing his or her unit. These items not only help ensure the success of the owner_tenant relationship, but also contribute to the successful operation of the association to which the investor_owner is a member.

All Owners Must:

1.   Give prior notice to the Board and/or management of their intention to lease, whereupon the Board should provide the unit owner a standard lease rider which should be added to the lease and signed by all parties executing the lease. Thereafter, the unit owner shall deliver a copy of the signed lease and lease rider to the Board or managing agent within ten days after it is executed and *prior to occupancy*.

2. Notify the association's Board of Directors or managing agent of all current occupants of the unit, including children. This notification should include not only the names of each occupant but the phone number of the unit, the number of vehicles used by the occupant(s), the number and type of any pets (if permitted) and so on.

3. Give all tenants a copy of the legal documents and any rules and regulations that have been adopted by the association's Board of Directors. Tenants should be informed that this information is being provided to them because they are a part of the association by virtue of their residency and are obligated to obey the provisions of the documents.

4. Advise all tenants regarding the operational structure of the association, that a portion of their rents is used to pay the monthly association assessments on the unit and what that assessment is used for. All tenants must sign the lease rider acknowledging receipt of copies of all legal documents.

5. Collect a security deposit sufficient to cover lost rent and/or damage, as well as the first month's rent.

6. Check out all previous landlords and credit references; verify information such as addresses, dates, etc.

7. Determine whether income is sufficient to pay rent without imposing a financial burden and whether income can accommodate any increase in the monthly assessment. Take into consideration existing debt obligations such as other

monthly payments, and what savings, reserves, or other resources are available to the applicant in case of a financial setback.

8. Make a final determination from a number of applicants rather than just one or two.
9. Avoid discrimination on the basis of age, race, color, creed, national origin, or sex.
10. Make a judgment on how long the tenant will likely stay. Turnover is costly; a minimum one year lease is required.
11. Pay all condominium fees. The unit owner is also obligated to pay all special assessments of the association, increase in taxes, move_in charges, maintenance costs, or any special fees or charges imposed by the association, since they are a covenant running with the land.

    Make sure the tenant has the following:

    A. Access to recreation and parking areas.
    B. Keys to mailbox and common areas.
    C. Community handbooks.
    D. Emergency numbers.
    E. Landlord address and telephone number.

13. Pay all fines, costs and legal fees incurred by the tenant. Any violations of the declaration, by-laws or the association's rules and regulations may result in a flat or daily fine, or in more serious situations, eviction proceedings.

All Leases Must:

1. Be in writing and for a period of not less than one year. All leases must be in conformance with, and make specific reference to, the legal documents of the association. Whether he or she

resides in the unit or not, the property owner is ultimately responsible for his or her tenants as to whether or not they abide by all provisions and restrictions imposed by the association's legal documents. If a tenant violates the documents or rules and regulations, the owner shall also be held responsible.

2. Include provisions for the tenant to acknowledge their responsibility to obey the by-laws, declaration and rules and regulations of the community, including the payment of any fines for rule violations, written legal termination procedure, penalties for late rent payment, method and location of rent payment, security deposit return and deduction procedure, with a written acknowledgment by the tenant that he or she has received and accepts all of the conditions.

Additionally, All Applicants for Rental and Tenants Should:

1. Complete the prescribed tenant application form. It is important to ensure that all the information necessary to make a good judgment on the qualifications of the applicant is ascertained in a timely fashion.

2. Participate in the committee structure of the association. Even though tenants have no vote on association matters, by virtue of their residence they are a part of the community and may be allowed and encouraged to participate in the association's activities.

Non-Compliance

The Board reserves the right to prohibit a tenant from occupying a unit until the owner complies with all leasing requirements. The Board reserves the right to initiate legal proceedings against the tenant and/or the owner for breach of any of the rules.

By maintaining strict policies governing the use and occupancy of the units, the Board will receive less complaints about tenants overall and will be better equipped to address specific problems.

CHAPTER 25

▼

EMPLOYMENT PRACTICES FOR ASSOCIATIONS AND MANAGEMENT

Many experts writing about association living often refer to it as the "new local government." In addition to exercising legislative and police powers, an association Board is also operating a business. Just as any other type of business, a Board must consider policies and procedures in dealing with contractors and in many instances, employees.

Initially, one must distinguish between an independent contractor, an employee and a volunteer. This is not always easy. How does one classify a Board member who makes it his or her job to change the light bulbs for no pay?

Anyone performing services for an association should be classified under a specific category, even if a written contract is not appropriate. Additionally, a written memorandum of the job description, scope of authority, compensation, etc. must be kept on file.

Although an association may take some measures to establish an independent contractor relationship, the law may not view it in that fashion. Many associations have people who are legally categorized as employees and are not even aware of it! That is why associations and management companies should have a fundamental understanding of their obligations and responsibilities in order to minimize risks of related liabilities.

Employee Rights

In recent years, Illinois has followed a trend away from guaranteeing employees a right to a job and has decreed that policy manuals and employment agreements govern the relationship. Employees without written contracts are considered "at will" and continue to be employed at the discretion of the employer. However, any written policies must be followed to the letter. Failure to do so can expose an employer to a claim for damages if an employee is "wrongfully terminated."

An association must be cautious in the initial hiring process. Inquiries cannot be made into any of the protected class areas (age, race, family status, etc.) and all hiring practices must be open and non-discriminatory. All interviews must focus on experience, ability and performance-related questions. Care should be taken to use an updated application form and the interviewer's comments should not be noted in writing.

Applicable Laws And Organizations

There are voluminous federal and state statutes and regulations governing rights of employees. Disputes arise primarily in instances of discrimination, injury and/or termination.

Every employer should make every effort to keep the workplace free from harm or hazardous substances. Cooperating with local governmental inspectors and insurance consultants should minimize the risks in this area. Injuries are common in the workplace and should be accepted as a cost of doing business, not a basis for instant termination.

Associations should be especially aware of their obligations under an agreement for collective bargaining, which is in effect on many properties, particularly for janitorial and maintenance personnel. If the association is not a party to a union contact, none of these laws would apply. If they do, an association and/or manager is cautioned to consult with a labor specialist before making any moves. Applicants and existing employees cannot be denied employment or advancement or be subjected to unreasonable disciplinary actions on the basis of race, age, sex, etc. Violating these very basic common sense guidelines would expose an employer to a civil rights claim, which is generally not covered by insurance.

Compensation

State law requires that employees working over 40 hours per week are entitled to "overtime" benefits of at least "time and a half," (150% of hourly rate after 40 hours). Professionals and administrative/management-type employees are exempted from these requirements. However, this law may apply to other types of personnel, i.e., bookkeepers, receptionists, etc. Also, any group subject to a collective bargaining agreement would also be excluded, subject to the terms of their contract.

Insurance

An employee that is injured on the job is entitled to reimbursement for lost wages and all medical expenses, and compensation for any disability. Injured employees are also entitled to occupational therapy, retraining and rehabilitation, depending upon the scope of the injury. If an employer does not have insurance, they are legally deemed self-insured. This issue comes up most often when an association opts not to purchase Worker's Compensation insurance. A diligent Board member and/or property manager should insist on this type of coverage for all associations. As previously stated, the law can deem certain individuals to be employees for liability purposes, when in all instances the Board considered them to be independent contractors. Further, even if the law views the worker as an employee, the IRS may not.

An employer is not required to offer health and disability insurance. However, if a plan is in place, it cannot be discriminatory; that is, all full time employees must have the same right to participate. Lastly, when an employee who is covered under a health insurance plan is terminated, the federal act known as COBRA (Comprehensive Omnibus Budget Reduction Act of 1985) requires the employer to keep the coverage in effect for 18 months or until replacement coverages are obtained (whichever is sooner).

Employment Agreements

For some employees, it is best to have the duties, terms and conditions of employment spelled out in a written contract. It is often difficult to resolve disputes when the issue of "covenants not to compete" are included. Even though employers may wish to restrict their employees from opening competing businesses in their backyard, these types of covenants are extremely difficult to enforce and should be drawn up by an attorney who is knowledgeable in this area. Otherwise, a court will look for any reason to throw it out.

Family Leave

The Family Leave Bill requires employers to release certain employees for up to 12 weeks to handle maternity, illness and other related matters, without penalty. This law applies to companies with 50 or more full-time employees and has certain exceptions. For the majority of associations and management companies, it is not applicable. In this instance, the employer can establish their own policy, so long as it is uniformly applied.

Americans With Disabilities Act (ADA)

This law compels employers to address the needs of employees or potential employees with disabilities. For companies with 15 or more employees, the Act prohibits discrimination in all phases of employment including hiring, firing, advancement, compensation, training, benefits, access, equipment, etc. For applicants and employees who become disabled, an employer must make reasonable accommodation to the workplace and equipment, so long as it does not impose an "undue hardship" on the operation of the business.

Since this is a relatively new area of law, it is important for managers and directors to check with legal counsel as to what provisions of the ADA apply to specific situations. However, many of these questions may remain unsettled until regulations and case law are available.

Termination Benefits

In Illinois, an employee is entitled to unemployment benefits if he or she is involuntarily unemployed (fired), able to work, actively seeking work and not subject to disqualification as a result of resignation, termination for misconduct or failure to accept suitable employment. Employees that quit for good cause can also be eligible for benefits so long as it is a protected category such as health reasons, sexual harassment, etc. Resignations "without good cause" can be protested by the employer.

Aside from the payment of benefits, an employer must be diligent in protecting itself from a wrongful termination claim. It is important that a file be maintained for each employee. Any incident of misconduct or poor performance should be noted in writing, with a copy given to the employee and preferably signed for as received. An employer should meet with an employee when a problem arises and note the nature and scope of the meeting in written form. Lastly, if enough incidents are accumulated where the employer needs to terminate the worker, an exit interview should be conducted. If a written employment or policy manual is in effect, all procedures must be followed to the letter.

Although the foregoing may not stop a wrongful discharge action from being filed, it should be sufficient to defeat any claim.

Lastly, accrued vacation, unpaid overtime, back wages, etc. should be paid promptly to avoid a complaint being filed with the Department of Labor.

Conclusion

By taking reasonable precautions in administering an association, or operating one's management business, employer liability claims can be avoided. By checking with qualified experts and legal counsel, other risks and liabilities can also be minimized. This will result in smoother operations as well as reduced insurance costs and legal fees.

CHAPTER 26

▼

BOARDS & MANAGERS:
PARTNERS OR ADVERSARIES

If you conducted a survey of association success stories and discovered a property that was perceived to be well-run, looked attractive and maintained a consistent level of property value appreciation, you would in all likelihood be talking about properties that have a close and harmonious relationship between the Board of Directors and the property manager.

The Board of Directors of a cooperative, condominium or a homeowner's association is a group of laypeople who are elected to the Board by other laypeople and whose only requirement for service is unit ownership. Obviously, intelligent, sensible people with good business instincts are case studies in good directors. However, Boards often consist of cross sections of all different types of people with

diverse personalities and backgrounds. If you add to this
equation the differences from manager to manager, this
relationship becomes an exercise in human interaction and
group dynamics.

The Role of the Board

The Board of Directors of a community association has
two distinct functions: (1) it is a Board of Directors of a
business, and (2) it is a legislative and enforcement body.

In performing their responsibilities as directors, members of the Board have the additional burden of acting as
fiduciaries on behalf of all of the members of the association. Board members must at all times use sound business
judgment, act in the best interests of the members of the
association, balance the budget, provide for contingencies,
preserve and protect the property and avoid acting outside
the scope of their authority as directors.

Although this can be an awesome list of duties, an efficient association can operate in all facets as a well-run
business with proper consultation and professional advice.
Since most people serving on a Board have little or no
expertise in running an association, most Boards will hire
a professional manager to advise and consult with for
advice in various areas.

The Role of the Manager

In practice, there are many theories about what a manager should be doing versus what tasks managers are actually required to perform.

Since the relationship between a manager and the
Board is that of a partnership, the underlying basis of the
relationship must be trust and confidence. Just as in the
case of an attorney and client, or a doctor and patient, if

the Board does not have total trust in its manager, then the relationship can never work.

A Board should hire a professional firm for its expertise and experience. A Board should not hire a professional to be its unemancipated slave.

A Manager Should

- Be available to the president or designated representative for consultation and advice on the administration of the property. Legal, accounting and structural problems should be referred to the appropriate professionals.

- Work with the Board to obtain, review and screen competitive bids on specifications prepared for various contractors.

- Periodically inspect the property and report any observable defects.

- Act as a liaison between the members of the association and the Board.

- Review the financial condition of the association and make recommendations regarding economic deficiencies and cost savings.

- Document all ongoing contractual relationships and advise the Board of renewals, cancellations and poor performance.

- Act as a go-between for the Board and it's attorney, accountant and other contractors.

- Assist the Board in running a controlled and professional business meeting.

- Be polite and professional with all persons.

- Provide the Board with a monthly update of activities handled by the management company.

- Present financial information prepared by the management company and be prepared to answer questions.
- Have work inspected by a third party prior to authorizing payment in full.

A Manager Should Not
- Be the police department.
- Prepare specifications, render legal advice or give accounting opinions.
- Be responsible for making sure there is toilet paper in the public bathrooms, etc.
- Be the sole signatory on a check.
- Have to get the consent of the Board to perform required tasks under the contract.
- Personally supervise contractors.
- Take direction from individual Board members or residents.
- Dictate policies without clear direction from the Board.

Three C's.

1.   **Confidence.** The Board of Directors needs to feel that the affairs of the association are being handled by a competent, experienced professional. When a management company sends a low-paid, inexperienced fledgling to manage millions of dollars worth of real property, the anxiety level on the Board runs very high.

When a director asks a question that is met by a stammer or unsure answer, the Board will want to be involved in every single matter. When this happens, there is no need to pay for a management company because the Board is duplicating the manager's job. When a Board feels compelled to "micro-manage" the property, they might as well self-manage.

2.   **Communication**. Open lines of communication between the manager and the president or Board liaison will solve a lot of problems. It is when people operate in a vacuum or cover up mistakes, problems arise. Sometimes it is okay to say "I made a mistake!"

Most important, at the beginning of the relationship and each year after the election, the manager should sit down with the Board and establish goals and objectives for the coming year. The Board must be frank and open about its expectations while the manager must set limits on what is included within the scope of the contract.

Free and open communication and written follow up will go a long way in curtailing misunderstandings or false expectations.

3.   **Cooperation**. The Board/manager relationship is a team effort. It should not be adversarial, and everyone must realize that they are working toward the same goals.

Conclusion

So long as both parties understand their respective roles and conduct themselves accordingly, the manager/Board relationship can be a rewarding and productive experience. Each year, new Board members or successor account managers need to be schooled in the same areas so as to keep the information flow steady and the relationship on a solid and professional level. The ultimate beneficiary will be the property owners, which is what this is really all about.

CHAPTER 27

▼

UMBRELLA ASSOCIATIONVS. RESIDENTIAL ASSOCIATION RESPONSIBILITY

One of the more routine tasks of an attorney who represents community associations is reviewing the governing documents of an association to advise the Board of Directors whether certain maintenance responsibilities belong to the unit owners or the association.

Frequently this type of analysis must be expanded to determine whether certain exterior repairs should be rendered by a master association versus an individual residential association. Usually the question can be resolved by reviewing the declarations and the various plats of survey. A conclusion can be drawn from comparing lot lines, legal descriptions, definition and descriptive language sections. When a dispute arises, the building exteriors or common areas then have to be apportioned for budgeting and assessment collection purposes. Sometimes the analysis becomes more complex and a "rule of reason" has to be applied.

An Illinois appeals court reviewed this issue in *Carl Sandburg Village Condominium Association No. 1 v. Carl Sandburg Village*, 175 Ill. App.3d 125 Ill. Dec. 122, 530 N.E.2d 40, 1987, and the opinion of the court provides some guidance for future disputes.

A problem arose between the individual condominium associations and the homeowner's association regarding maintenance responsibility for concrete columns supporting underground parking garage roofs. The controversy arose over interpretation of the distinction between concrete structures, referred to as "malls," and their relationship to "community facilities." The entire association consists of nine condominium buildings, 60 townhouses and recreational facilities connected by a series of unenclosed walks, malls, paths, driveways and public streets. The malls are underground and the ceilings of the garages form the bottom of the malls. Townhome owners do not have garages, which are owned by the individual condominium owners as tenants in common, each owning a respective percentage.

The trial court had determined that there was no issue of fact and cited previous authority that the interpretation of a condominium declaration is purely a matter of law. (*Damen Savings & Loan Assoc. v. Johnson*, 126 Ill. App.3d 940, 944, 467 N.E.2d 1139, 1984; *LaSalle National Bank v. Triumvera Homeowners Association*, 109 Ill. App.3d 654, 661, 440 N.E.2d 1073, 1982.)

The court held that the homeowners association, not the condominium association, was responsible for maintenance of the malls since the malls include wearing surfaces, garage roof slabs, support columns, expansion joints, etc., which were all part of the "community facilities."

On appeal, the court reasoned that it was required to apply Solomonic logic: "Since portions of these completely integrated concrete structures are common to both the garages and the malls they can fairly be said to be 'claimed' by both."

Thus, the first issue, arriving at a definition of what constituted a "mall" versus a "concrete structure," was hotly disputed. Once the court resolved that a "mall" was a component of the "community facilities," the next task was to determine that the homeowners association declaration granted exclusive authority to the association to provide exterior maintenance and services with respect to the "community facilities."

Unfortunately, after its analysis of conflicting language in the homeowners association and condominium documents, the court stated, "We find no clear answer to the question of whether the concrete structures are considered part of the malls." The significant concept which determined the final outcome of its decision is the question of "usage."

Since the homeowners association declaration demonstrated that the intention of the declarant was that the "community facilities be used by and be available to **all residents**," then the concrete structures are under the dominion of the homeowners association, while the malls of the parking garages are controlled by, and therefore should be repaired by, the individual condominium associations.

Since the townhome owners do not have access to or an interest in the parking garages, the court interpreted the definition of "community facilities" to exclude the garages from this definition.

Therefore, when determining the issues of maintenance responsibility, the legal opinion must first be based on the authority of the governing statute and the operating documents. When the definition is not expressed in clear and precise language, then the ultimate user(s) must be established. This will then be the deciding factor. This rule of reason can be applied not just in the instance of a homeowners association versus residential association conflicts, but also in residential associations versus individual owner conflicts as well.

The concept of "limited common elements" was created as a result of this same philosophy in limiting a condominium association's maintenance responsibility, and now this Illinois case provides further insight into this extremely complex area of law.

In conclusion, when there is a dispute between a residential association and a master association over maintenance responsibility and the documents are silent, "who" uses the facility will determine the final answer.

CHAPTER 28

▼

MAN'S BEST FRIEND? THE ASSOCIATION'S WORST ENEMY

One of the most serious and annoying problems confronting the Board of Directors at a cooperative, condominium or townhome association is dealing with pet violations.

Subject to the restrictions imposed by local municipalities, keeping a pet in one's home within a common interest community is generally allowed unless specifically prohibited or limited by a restrictive covenant. Such covenants are often found in the declaration of condominium or townhome associations. Whether or not the owners actually know of the covenant does not matter. A properly recorded declaration and/or any amendments are constructive notice to all owners, and an owner takes title to his or her unit subject to these restrictions.

Adding or Eliminating Restrictive Covenants

The members of an association can either add a "no pet" clause or remove an existing restriction through an amendment to the declaration. If a declaration expressly or implicitly allows pets, then this is a vested property right which can be eliminated only by a valid amendment. A modification of the rules and regulations is simply not adequate.

In 1978, one of the first cases on the subject upheld the principle that a vested property right, such as the right to own and maintain a pet, may not be retroactively abolished by a mere rule change. (*Winston Towers 200 Assn. Inc. v. Saverio*, Fla. 3d Dist. Ct. and *Movighes v. Playa Del Sol Assn., Inc.*, also a Florida third District case from 1978.) These cases also established the principle of "grandfather" clauses for pet amendments.[4]

Each declaration and/or by-laws set forth the requirements to implement amendments. For some associations, a meeting may not be necessary if the declaration provides for approval by a certain percentage of the membership in writing on an instrument setting forth the proposed terms.

However, any amendment which does restrict the ability of an owner to keep pets must be sensitive to the needs of the pet owners at the time the amendment is approved. Conversely, on the rare occasion an association wishes to proceed with an amendment which liberalizes pet restrictions, it should take into consideration the needs of those members who purchased their units in reliance on these

---

4. A "grandfather" clause requires that any change of an existing condition that materially affects a vested property right, must allow the condition to continue until it expires by either a change of condition of attrition (e.g., the death of a pet).

restrictions. Neither of these circumstances is easy to handle and no solution will be completely satisfactory.

"Grandfathering" or "depreciation" are concepts which must be used when pet ownership provisions become more restrictive. Pets which are currently on the premises are allowed to remain with their owners but cannot be replaced. When the provisions are amended to become less restrictive, the effective date should be set far enough in the future so that adversely affected owners can attempt to sell their units and minimize their hardship.

However, as in the case of any amendment, when a person buys a unit in a common interest community, he or she should be aware that the "power to amend" can change the quality of life at any time.

Enforcement of Restrictive Covenants

Once a valid restrictive covenant is in place, the regulation of pets can be accomplished by means of effective, thorough rules and enforcement procedures. An accused resident must be given proper notice of an alleged violation and an opportunity to be heard as to the allegations before any punitive measures can be taken. If the owner does not take advantage of an opportunity to present evidence about the incident or defend his or her point of view, the hearing should be held nonetheless. This is a basic principle of "due process of law" found in the United States and state constitutions. The Illinois Condominium Property Act, §18.4(e) *et seq.*, requires hearings and notice prior to the levy of any fine.

Rules governing pets should define the term "pet" specifically and spell out those types of animals which are not included. Species, size and behavioral restrictions should be set forth clearly. Remedies and procedures for any violation should be distinct and straight forward.

Notice and hearing procedures should also all be spelled out in detail in the association rules. A Board can jeopardize its ability to enforce rules by failing to apply them consistently and uniformly. Established policy and procedures must not stray from any explicit provisions contained in the declaration or by-laws and the rules and regulations.

Local Government Enforcement

Once a hearing has been conducted and a finding has been rendered or when there is a widespread problem that cannot be punished because of lack of proof, the local authorities should be consulted.

Most municipalities, or the county in unincorporated areas, have health and zoning regulations pertaining to animal control. By filing a complaint and appearing in court, the association can force the notorious pet violator to suffer criminal prosecution with the cooperation of the local policing authorities. This is an effective remedy without the association expending legal fees.

Conclusion

The most effective way to deal with irresponsible pet owners is to have tough rules and regulations and strict enforcement procedures. This will allow the association to solve a constant and annoying problem, yet deal with its membership in a fair and conscientious fashion.

CHAPTER 29

▼

PROCEDURES FOR CONDUCTING INFORMAL AND ADMINISTRATIVE HEARINGS FOR COOPERATIVES, CONDOMINIUMS AND HOMEOWNERS ASSOCIATIONS

I. The Illinois Condominium Property Act [§18.4(1)] requires that before a fine can be levied, a unit owner must receive notice and is entitled to a hearing. However, any association must implement due process of law procedures before utilizing its police powers.

II. In order to provide a fair and impartial hearing for all residents accused of rules violations, the following procedures should be adopted by the Board:

A. Standard form violation notice should be made available for complaints. Owners and/or the manager should send these to the Board when reporting rule violations.

B. Upon receipt, the Board must notify the accused resident that a complaint has been filed. The Board can establish a policy that all complaints are first dealt with by sending a warning letter.

C. The Board should appoint a hearing committee consisting of 3-5 people. At least one director should serve on the committee. The remaining members should be non-Board members, if possible. Of course, if the complaining witness is a director or committee member, he or she must remove themselves from the proceedings.

D. A notice must be sent to the accused owner (and tenant, where applicable), advising the nature of the violation(s) and the time and place where a hearing will be convened.

E. The hearing should commence on the date, time and place as set forth in the notice, unless a request for a continuance is made well in advance of the date and is approved by the hearing panel.

F. Failure of any party or witness to appear will not delay or cancel a hearing unless the Board has been notified in advance of a request for a postponement and there is sufficient time for the Board to notify all parties of the new date.

G. The hearing panel should designate a chairman. The Board reserves the right to appoint any individual to the committee or as chairman, including the association attorney. The chairman will direct the proceedings and strictly follow the agenda. Any person who has an interest in the case, such as a complainant, shall also be excluded from the panel.

H.   The hearing should commence whether or not the parties appear at the specified date and time. At the commencement of the hearing, the chairman should set a time limit on all proceedings and the entire length of the hearing itself, e.g.:

1.   20 minutes total.

2.   Complaining witness statements and reading of complaints and letters—5 minutes.

3.   Accused's statements and questioning of witnesses—5 minutes.

4.   Questions by committee of witnesses and accused—5 minutes.

5.   Final statements:
a. Accused—2 minutes
b. Complaining witness— 2 minutes
c. Committee—1 minute

I.   After all testimony has been heard and all questions asked by the panel, the hearing should then be adjourned and all parties excused. The committee can then recommend a fine, legal action, a strong letter of warning or a finding of not guilty to the Board of Directors.

J.   The committee should deliberate in private and prepare a recommendation to be given to the Board of Directors to be reviewed and voted on at the next regularly scheduled Board meeting.

K.   The Board votes to either accept, reject or modify the recommendations of the committee and the Board's findings should be recorded in the minutes.

L.   After the Board meeting, the Board's findings are sent to the accused in writing, with copies to complaining witnesses.

M.   Minutes should be kept of all proceedings. Although the records of a proceeding to enforce the rules should not be open to inspection by any other owner, a complete file, with a full "paper trail" should be maintained by the Board in the event of litigation. However, if people are afforded due process of law and the hearing is fair and impartial, there will be few claims and no basis to challenge the proceedings.

Conclusion

Meetings have become a way of life (as evidenced by my vanity plate "MEETING"). The keys to having successful meetings are organization and conciseness. The keys to a successful association are organized and concise meetings. It is my hope that the thinking expressed in this book is a practical day-to-day guidebook for the operation of the association. The well run association will accomplish the ultimate goal—preservation and appreciation of property values.

Association living is a valuable way of life. It provides a shared living experience for many people. It has the potential to reduce living expenses through commonly assessed maintenance. It provides affordable housing for millions of people. It is the ultimate exercise in democracy.

Since it is a relatively new lifestyle for most people and has really only taken hold since the 1960's, there are still many more things to learn.

I hope this book has given you an overview of some of the basics and will help you and your Association become a better place to live.

The Author

About the Author

Jordan Shifrin is a graduate of the John Marshall Law School and has been practicing law since 1977. Raised in Chicago, he attended the University of Illinois at Chicago and received his Bachelor and Master of Arts in History.

Prior to becoming a lawyer, he was a public school teacher.

Author of numerous articles and lecturer on dozens of topics, has helped the law firm of Kovitz Shifrin & Waitzman of which he is a founding partner, to develop a regional reputation.

Jordan lives in Buffalo Grove with his wife and two children and loves reading history, playing softball and collecting toy soldiers.

www.ingramcontent.com/pod-product-compliance
Lightning Source LLC
Chambersburg PA
CBHW020913290526
45784CB00002BA/539